AFRICAN KINGDOMS

TIME
LIFE
BOOKS
®

LIFE WORLD LIBRARY

LIFE NATURE LIBRARY

TIME READING PROGRAM

THE LIFE HISTORY OF THE UNITED STATES

LIFE SCIENCE LIBRARY

GREAT AGES OF MAN

TIME-LIFE LIBRARY OF ART

TIME-LIFE LIBRARY OF AMERICA

FOODS OF THE WORLD

THIS FABULOUS CENTURY

LIFE LIBRARY OF PHOTOGRAPHY

THE TIME-LIFE ENCYCLOPEDIA OF GARDENING

FAMILY LIBRARY
　THE TIME-LIFE BOOK OF FAMILY FINANCE
　THE TIME-LIFE FAMILY LEGAL GUIDE

GREAT AGES OF MAN

A History of the World's Cultures

AFRICAN KINGDOMS

by

BASIL DAVIDSON

and

The Editors of TIME-LIFE BOOKS

TIME-LIFE BOOKS, NEW YORK

THE AUTHOR: Basil Davidson is a distinguished English author and Africanist who has traveled widely through the continent since 1951. Among his books on contemporary affairs are: *The African Awakening* and *Which Way Africa?*; his historical works include *The Lost Cities of Africa*, *Black Mother*, *The African Past* and *Africa: History of a Continent*. He has written four novels, one of which, *The Rapids*, describes the rise of nationalism in a country similar to Angola.

THE CONSULTING EDITOR: Leonard Krieger, now Professor of History at Columbia University, was formerly Professor of History at Yale. Dr. Krieger is the author of *The German Idea of Freedom* and *Politics of Discretion*, and co-author of *History*, written in collaboration with John Higham and Felix Gilbert.

THE COVER: The Oba, or King, of Benin, carrying his ceremonial hammer, is seen on one of a group of bronze plaques that form a treasure of early African art.

TIME-LIFE BOOKS

FOUNDER: Henry R. Luce 1898-1967

EDITOR-IN-CHIEF: Hedley Donovan
CHAIRMAN OF THE BOARD: Andrew Heiskell
PRESIDENT: James R. Shepley
CHAIRMAN, EXECUTIVE COMMITTEE: James A. Linen
EDITORIAL DIRECTOR: Louis Banks

VICE CHAIRMAN: Roy E. Larsen

EDITOR: Jerry Korn
EXECUTIVE EDITOR: A. B. C. Whipple
PLANNING DIRECTOR: Oliver E. Allen
TEXT DIRECTOR: Martin Mann
ART DIRECTOR: Sheldon Cotler
CHIEF OF RESEARCH: Beatrice T. Dobie
DIRECTOR OF PHOTOGRAPHY: Melvin L. Scott
Associate Planning Director: Byron Dobell
Assistant Text Directors: Ogden Tanner, Diana Hirsh
Assistant Art Director: Arnold C. Holeywell
Assistant Chief of Research: Martha T. Goolrick

PUBLISHER: Joan D. Manley
General Manager: John D. McSweeney
Business Manager: John Steven Maxwell
Sales Director: Carl G. Jaeger
Promotion Director: Paul R. Stewart
Public Relations Director: Nicholas Benton

GREAT AGES OF MAN

SERIES EDITOR: Russell Bourne
Editorial Staff for *African Kingdoms:*
Assistant Editors: Carlotta Kerwin, Betsy Frankel
Text Editors: Ogden Tanner, Harvey B. Loomis
Picture Editor: Jean Tennant
Designer: Norman Snyder
Assistant Designer: Ladislav Svatos
Staff Writers: Timothy Carr, Sam Halper,
Jonathan Kastner, Lucille Schulberg, Edmund White
Chief Researcher: Thelma C. Stevens
Researchers: Alice Baker, Barbara Ballantine,
Kathleen Brandes, Mary W. Constant,
Patricia Huntington, Frank Kendig, Jeffrey Tarter,
Johanna Zacharias

EDITORIAL PRODUCTION
Production Editor: Douglas B. Graham
Quality Director: Robert L. Young
Assistant: James J. Cox
Copy Staff: Rosalind Stubenberg,
Patricia Miller, Florence Keith
Picture Department: Dolores A. Littles,
Joan Lynch
Art Assistants: Anne Landry, Robert Pellegrini

The following Time Inc. individuals and departments helped prepare this book: Editorial Production, Norman Airey, Margaret T. Fischer; Library, Peter Draz; Picture Collection, Doris O'Neil; Photographic Laboratory, George Karas; TIME-LIFE News Service, Murray J. Gart; Correspondents Elisabeth Kraemer (Bonn), Traudl Lessing (Vienna), Ann Natanson (Rome), Katharine Sachs, Barbara Moir (London), Maria Vincenza Aloisi, Joan Dupont (Paris), Ato Mogus Tekle-Mikael (Addis Ababa), Ann Turner (Nairobi).

CONTENTS

INTRODUCTION 7

Prelude: THE CHALLENGE OF THE LAND 8

1 THE HIDDEN CITIES 16
Picture Essay: TRAVELERS' SPLENDROUS TALES 23

2 CIVILIZATIONS OF THE NILE 32
Picture Essay: THE OLDEST AFRICANS 43

3 THE TRADITION OF THE TRIBE 58
Picture Essay: THE WRESTLERS 67

4 MERCHANT EMPIRES 78
Picture Essay: A NETWORK OF COMMERCE 89

5 FOREST KINGDOMS 100
Picture Essay: THE METROPOLIS OF BENIN 109

6 GODS AND SPIRITS 120
Picture Essay: CHURCHES HEWN FROM ROCK 129

7 ARTS THAT CAPTURE LIFE 142
Picture Essay: VIGOROUS SHAPES IN WOOD 151

8 A CONTINENT TRIUMPHANT 166
Picture Essay: THE ENDURING FORMS 175

Chronologies 184
Bibliography, credits and art notes 186
Acknowledgments 187
Index 188

INTRODUCTION

When the peoples of Europe overflowed into the rest of the world between the 16th and 19th Centuries, the indigenous populations of most colonized lands went under. Indians in America and aborigines in Australia had not sufficiently tamed and filled their continents to prevent newcomers from settling among them and multiplying at a rate much faster than their own. Within two or three centuries the original populations of these two continents were reduced to insignificant minorities.

Faced with the same challenge, the Africans survived. Only in the southern tip of their continent, where an uncultivated corner had been left in the hands of hunters and food-gatherers, did European migrants succeed in establishing a self-propagating community. Elsewhere Africans were too numerous and too much the masters of their environment to be overtaken. Subject to alien rule for a brief period during the late 19th and early 20th Centuries, they were nowhere outnumbered, nor was their culture destroyed.

Surely this must mean that Africans are worth studying; surely their achievement is not without interest to their fellow men. If the history of Africa seems a jungle, it is more likely a jungle of ignorance. Through it, paths are even now being cut, and one of the foremost pathfinders is Basil Davidson. As a writer rather than a professional scholar, Davidson has escaped what is both the virtue and the temptation of the latter—the desire to mark out a single square mile of virgin forest for his very own and cut it down tree by tree. On the contrary, Davidson has made it his business to look in on other men's clearings and report their discoveries with fairness and generosity. His learning is large and liberal. Few have read so widely into the written sources of African history. Few have so thoroughly mastered the findings of archeology and anthropology, and presented them in a way that commands the respect of the experts.

In this volume he attempts a bold synthesis: to draw the fruits of anthropological research into the field of historical vision, and thus explore not only the large centralized states that once existed in Africa, but also the past of its simple village societies. The history of these societies can only be presented by taking examples from the present and weaving into them impressions and reflections gained from the wider story. It is perilous work, but to sidestep it is to ignore one whole facet of African life and achievement.

Some readers may feel that in evaluating the African past Davidson tends to be romantic and eulogistic. They may be assured that this is a matter of interpretation, not invention; Davidson commands his sources. If he assesses them too admiringly for some tastes, he also rights an old imbalance. Certainly he is one of the very few outsiders whose writings enjoy the real confidence of Africans and serious students of Africa.

ROLAND OLIVER
Professor of African History
University of London

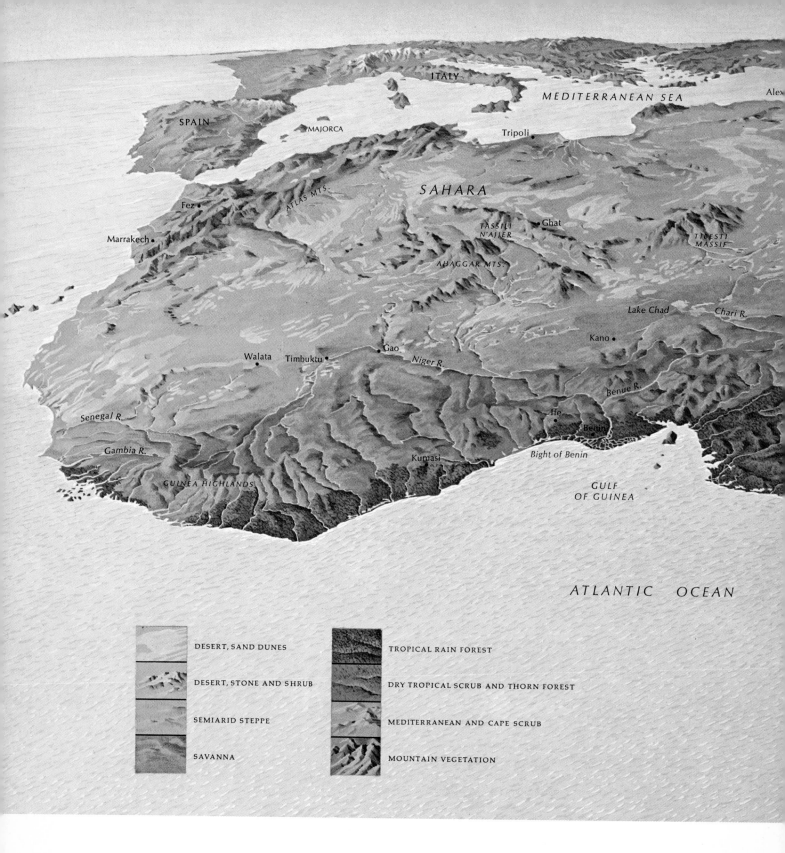

DESERT, SAND DUNES	TROPICAL RAIN FOREST
DESERT, STONE AND SHRUB	DRY TROPICAL SCRUB AND THORN FOREST
SEMIARID STEPPE	MEDITERRANEAN AND CAPE SCRUB
SAVANNA	MOUNTAIN VEGETATION

THE CHALLENGE OF THE LAND

The peoples of Africa have been called "small figures in an immense scenery." Immense it is indeed: Africa is the world's second-largest continent in area. It is a domain of harsh beauty, sometimes terrifying emptiness and unparalleled topographic extremes. To understand this land is to begin to understand how and why the African kingdoms of history grew.

The geography of Africa, as this map shows, follows an

his
Nile R.
Mecca •
RED SEA
GULF OF ADEN
NUBIAN DESERT
Napata •
• Meroë
ARFUR
Khartoum •
Axum •
Lalibela •
ETHIOPIAN HIGHLANDS
SOMALI PENINSULA
INDIAN OCEAN
N
SUDD
RIFT VALLEY
RUWENZORI RANGE
Lake Victoria
LAMU
Malindi
Mombasa
ZANZIBAR
Congo R.
← KILWA
Lake Tanganyika
Lake Malawi (Nyasa)
MOZAMBIQUE CHANNEL
Congo R.
Kasai R.
MADAGASCAR
Zambezi R.
Zimbabwe •
• Sofala
← Victoria Falls
Limpopo R.
KALAHARI DESERT
Vaal R.
NAMIB DESERT
Orange R.
DRAKENSBERG MTS.
CAPE OF GOOD HOPE
David Greenspan

orderly pattern, beginning with strips of fertile land at both ends. These soon expire into dull brown emptiness: the vast Kalahari Desert in the south, and in the north the still vaster *Sahra,* the ancient Arabic name echoing the sound of a parched man's gasp for water. Bordering the deserts are narrow, more hospitable bands of shrub and bush forest and rolling grassland. Then comes the great tropical rain forest,

once aptly described as a "glittering equatorial slum [where] huge trees jostle one another for room to live."

Some of these extremes of nature are suggested in the pictorial prelude that follows. They are only a few of the contrasts of Africa, a land that has long held man back in awe of it—yet in certain favored spots has beckoned him to bring forth nations of splendid traditions and ancient grandeur.

In much of Africa, nature has defied man's attempts to settle and civilize the land. There are many mountains that disappear upward into drenching, uninhabitable cloud forest, and some, like the Ruwenzori Range (far left), that soar above 16,500 feet, perpetually capped by snow and ice. The dark expanse of the equatorial forest (left) covers nearly a million square miles; its rain-leached soil offers a poor living to man. In the Sahara's broad ocean of trackless, burning dunes (below) nothing lives at all.

The grassy savanna is the best part of Africa; here,
through the ages, men have built clusters of huts—
communities which are the nucleus of African civilization.

Relics of grandeur—2,200-year-old pyramids of Kush, Africa's oldest and greatest inland empire—stand on a once-fer

ain in the Sudan.

1
THE HIDDEN CITIES

For many centuries Africa and its people seemed mysterious and even perverse to the rest of the world. Generations of traders anchored their ships off the continent's glittering surf line and pushed their caravans through its dry, abrasive plains. They knew and valued Africa's gold and ivory, but the continent itself remained a puzzle. Where had Africans come from? Why were they so different from other men? What was the explanation for their strange customs, so unlike those of Europe?

Many answers were proposed, but most of them served only to deepen the darkness that surrounded the image of Africa. At last the Europeans resorted to an easy conclusion—one that reflected their inability to judge any culture except in terms of their own. Africans, they decided, were just savages, inferior beings, and had always been so.

This simple-minded answer to the riddle of Africa has lasted right up to modern times. Recently, however, in one of the great intellectual adventures of the 20th Century, Africa has been rediscovered by the scholars. Probing into the obscure past, they have turned up fascinating information. Africa has not been, after all, a land of unrelieved savagery and chaos. On the contrary, its people have had a long and lively history, and have made an impressive contribution to man's general mastery of the world. They have created cultures and civilizations, evolved systems of government and systems of thought, and pursued the inner life of the spirit with a consuming passion that has produced some of the finest art known to man.

The early explorers sometimes glimpsed these truths, seeing what other men afterward forgot. In 1498, Vasco da Gama and his Portuguese sailors, having thrust their small ships down through the South Atlantic and around the Cape of Good Hope, were gladdened to come upon tall stone towns of comfort and wealth along the East African coast. They went ashore to find a people who knew as much about charts and compasses as they did, and were sometimes more civilized; the Portuguese were repeatedly snubbed for being uncouth.

Twenty years later Pope Leo X in Rome was astonished to learn from a captured Moor that the legendary city of Timbuktu, far beyond the southern skyline, had many scholars—so many, in fact,

THE QUEEN MOTHER OF BENIN, *one of the most advanced cities, and civilizations, in African history, is depicted in this 16th Century bronze sculpture. Her tall, beaded headdress and many necklaces are marks of her position.*

that its merchants made a greater profit from books than from any other commodity. The merchants of Holland heard similar reports about other places. Buskined Dutchmen, sweating through the rain forests of Nigeria, came upon the civic splendor of the city of Benin. Its streets, they told their employers back home, were as wide as those of Amsterdam; its king lived in a palace that occupied "as much space as the town of Haarlem."

News of this kind continued to find its way to Europe. But the early European travelers seldom went far inland and the descriptions of the places they visited were never more than fragmentary. Often they embellished their tales with myths and monsters drawn from European folklore. Just as often they told of strange customs that seemed stranger still for lack of adequate explanation—few of the travelers understood enough of any of the African languages to ask questions about what they saw or to comprehend the answers. In time their stories were either forgotten or were borrowed and used by other men to provide catchpenny sensations for popular audiences. Since most of these borrowers were mainly interested in the lurid details, the hidden continent became even more mysterious, and its peoples even more strange. Africans were believed to be monsters, with souls as black as their skin. It was solemnly reported that they cooked and ate each other, gave birth in litters, like dogs, and sometimes did not even look like the rest of the human race: in one account there are Africans "without heads . . . having their eyes and mouth in their breast."

Shorn of all this frenzied embroidery, the older travelers' tales had some basis in fact. Placed against an ever-widening collection of information about Africa, they take on fresh meaning. Vasco da Gama and his men thought they had stumbled upon a string of Moorish cities set down inexplicably on a savage coast. In reality they had come upon the inheritors of an essentially African culture formed many centuries before. Even more impressive, it was a culture that depended for much of its life and vigor upon trade with other equally well-established African civilizations, far inland.

The captured Moor who entertained the Pope with tales of Timbuktu's book trade was not merely spinning tales to please his distinguished audience. On the contrary, his information was common knowledge to many men—although not to men in Europe. By the time the Moor saw Timbuktu it had been a center of commerce and learning for over 100 years, and was one of a number of similar cities in a group of large and powerful West African kingdoms. Two of the many scholars who supported Timbuktu's flourishing book trade wrote careful chronicles about them that are now indispensable sources of information on West African history.

In short, the tales of early travelers are now part of a much larger body of information coming from many sides. Some of this information emerges from the digging of archeologists in a dozen African countries. Some of it surfaces from a vast reservoir of unwritten but remembered history accumulated by many African peoples. Some of it develops from the piecing together of written records made long ago in Africa itself, in Arab cities of the Middle East, in Christian and Muslim cities of Europe, and in lands more distant still—as far away as China.

Even from this still-unfinished reconstruction, it is clear that the continent has had a long and fruitful record of achievement. Beneath its often primitive surface lay a profound and complicated cultural development. Far from being the helpless victims of their own ignorance, Africans had actually gone far toward taming their continent long before Europeans appeared on the scene. This achievement, so essential to survival, rested upon social and cultural advances of great antiquity. Africans conquered their environment out of bitter necessity and in the

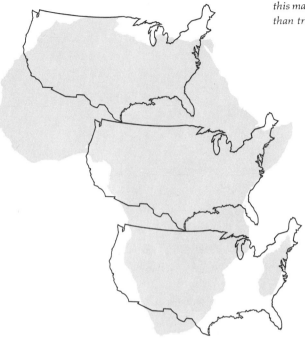

Not much is known or perhaps ever can be known about these less-than-fully-human men and women. But the present state of knowledge suggests that by about a million years ago they had become more numerous and different in type. From then until about 60,000 years ago, when man there had controlled fire, they and other creatures like them spread through the greater part of Africa. At that point the more successful of them settled down to reproducing a few fairly stable types. It seems likely that the basic differences in skin color, bone structure and the like were established some 30,000 years ago, although the movements of countless thousands of generations since then have blurred the contrasts. At the same time some differences have probably been emphasized by changes in the African climate, which periodically varied—with the shifting polar ice caps—from very wet to very dry.

The climatic period that matters most in the development of modern Africa, however, dates from about 5500 B.C. Between that time and about 2500 B.C., the continent's climate went from dry to wet, turning the upper half of Africa into a well-watered prairie. The present Sahara and the dry savannas were lush and green; mountains were clothed in fine trees, fish and game were plentiful. Here, in an area that was probably about the size of the continental United States, lay one of the principal nurseries of later African culture. Many generations of hunters, and later of farmers and herdsmen, roamed these broad plains and found shelter in the caves of the hills. Archeologists have recently begun to reconstruct the lives of these peoples through the mute evidence of hundreds of superb rock paintings which they left behind.

Then, about 4,000 years ago, the climate changed again. Little by little the rivers dwindled, the grass gave way to scrub and sand, the forests died. Nothing was left but fossilized seeds and a handful of

face of formidable obstacles, but they did not do it by physical means alone. Like all peoples everywhere they depended upon spiritual values, and these spiritual values enabled Africans to build close-knit societies without which they might have perished. Thus Africa's evolution was inspired by forces comparable to those that inspire every other branch of the human family.

The beginning of this evolution lies unthinkably far away: it appears that Africa may have been the birthplace of mankind. From the evidence of fossil skulls and bone fragments found in the last few decades, some of man's most remote ancestors apparently inhabited the high inland plains of eastern Africa almost two million years ago. The most famous fossil site is the Olduvai Gorge in northern Tanzania, where, in a climate thought to have been much as it is today, ancient beings learned to shape and use tools and weapons of stone, and hunted many kinds of game. Little groups of them appear to have lived together in temporary encampments.

ANOPHELES MOSQUITO   TSETSE FLY

stunted trees in a howling, sand-blown wilderness. The game and fish went, and the people inevitably followed. They dispersed in three directions, taking with them their memories, their customs and their gods. For some the road led north into the Mediterranean coastlands, where they merged with the local peoples to form the Berber culture. Others, later to be known as Libyans, settled in the fertile land along the Nile, and eventually supplied some of the princes who reigned over southern Egypt. Still others pushed slowly southward into the heart of the continent, where presumably they merged with indigenous peoples. Who these peoples were is a mystery. Bushmen and Pygmies seem to have been in Africa since very early times, but the ancestors of the modern Negro apparently emerged much later.

The Sahara's long climatic disaster, with its consequences of human movement, helps to explain why the history of Africa, after about 2000 B.C., goes in two different directions. The desert, except for a few intrepid travelers who continued to cross it by horse and then by camel, remained a daunting barrier. North of it emerged the high civilization of Egypt, nourishing and nourished by an interchange of ideas with the whole Mediterranean community. South of it people worked out their destiny alone. Their history is a record of accomplishments achieved in isolation against tremendous odds; it is a record that can be understood only against the background of the physical environment.

Sub-Saharan Africa is immense, 3,500 miles from north to south and 2,000 miles from east to west at its narrow, southern end. Vast though it is, very little of it is hospitable to man. The landscape has variety—wide grasslands, tall mountains, broad rivers, deep forests—but none of these land types is especially helpful to man. The grasslands are not lush prairies, but tropical savannas. Baked by six months of relentless sun, then leached by six months of heavy rains, their topsoil is soon stripped of its nutrients, and will grow only low-yield crops. The mountains that rise from these impoverished plains are beguilingly green—but with scrub and thorn, seldom with grass; their harsh skylines are almost constantly veiled in curtains of intense heat.

The broad rivers of Africa meander idly for hundreds of miles, then suddenly crash in tremendous falls that seem to split the earth wide open. Few of them are navigable very far inland, and almost none of them offers a direct and easy route from point to point. The forests are a dense and dank world where it rains up to eight feet a year, and a man can wander for days with only fleeting glimpses of the sun. There are also other discouragements. Much of the wide middle region of the continent has been infested since earliest times by the tsetse fly, a carrier of sleeping sickness among men and a comparable fever among their cattle. Riverbanks and plains alike are plagued by the malaria-carrying mosquito. And there is yellow fever.

Yet Africans overcame these obstacles. They conquered and peopled their inhospitable land, and carried their life and culture from one phase of social organization to another. They developed

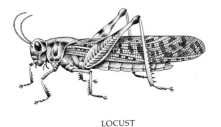

LOCUST

THREE INSECT VILLAINS were largely responsible for keeping Africa a dark, unknown continent for many years. The anopheles mosquito, breeding in watery areas, carries malaria, still Africa's most devastating disease. The tsetse fly, bearer of sleeping sickness, has not only killed thousands of Africans, but in many areas has made it impossible to keep domestic animals. Locusts, attacking every decade or so, can consume entire crops in minutes.

methods for growing crops and raising cattle; they learned how to extract metals from the earth and refine and use them. Armed with iron spears, they pressed through the trackless forests out into the hills and game-filled plains. They forged new ways of making a living and of living together. They settled in chosen places for ever-lengthening periods and in ever-increasing numbers. Most astonishing, they founded cities and built states and empires.

All of this took time—by modern standards of progress, a long time. Up to about 500 B.C. people south of the Sahara continued to live in Stone Age simplicity, few in number and always on the move in search of food. Then came a second phase, marked by a momentous discovery: how to mine, refine and work metals, especially iron. This occurred about the time of the birth of Christ. With iron-tipped tools and weapons, the tides of progress were unleashed. Farming became easier, and hunting a less precarious operation. Larger and more dependable food supplies encouraged the growth of populations, and of more complex societies. Communities that became too populous to feed themselves on a given area of land separated, going off to find new land and start new communities.

Shifting back and forth across the continent, colliding and mingling with each other, then moving off to form new groups, these migrants soon dominated the whole central and southern part of Africa. They ousted the backward Bushmen and Pygmies, and gave Africa a huge family of related languages, the Bantu, which today are spoken over most of the continent south of the equator. In the process

they created a complicated and diversified culture. Africans, who eventually spoke more than a thousand different tongues, had almost as many systems of behavior and belief. Some of these systems produced societies whose standard of living—in terms of food, personal safety and freedom—equaled that of contemporary societies in Europe. In some instances they were even more advanced: African societies practiced a simple but effective social welfare in their concern for widows and orphaned children.

This is the Africa—often called historical, or traditional Africa—that Muslims wrote about in the Ninth and 10th Centuries, and that Europeans began to see for themselves in the latter half of the 15th Century. Instead of a primeval wilderness, these visitors found prosperous, self-contained cities linked to each other by a busy, carefully ordered trade. Their inhabitants—merchants, artisans, laborers, clerks—lived comfortable lives. Their pleasures were the familiar ones cherished by all people —feasting and family gatherings. Africa was in many ways no more savage than Europe—at the time just concluding the Hundred Years' War and only recently occupied with burning Joan of Arc.

But in spite of this, marvelous or merely absurd tales about Africa continued to circulate in Europe. There were several reasons why. One was the secrecy practiced by royal chanceries and business houses, which were reluctant to publish, for the benefit of rivals, what they now began to know about the lands beyond the seas. A second was the dishonesty of literary hacks who concocted all sorts of nonsense for a gullible public. A third reason was the debasing effect of the slave trade. The records of the slaving centuries are full of references to Africans as "children who never grew up," and of paternalistic assurances about the good that was being done for them by non-Africans. Out of this carefully nurtured misconception came the great theme of the colonial epoch, the idea of "the white man's burden."

But there was also a fourth reason why Europe continued to misjudge Africa. Africans were different. They were a different color, they dressed differently and, probably most important of all, their values were different. To Europeans beginning to be caught up in an age of machinery and science, it was easy to assume that Africa's technological simplicity was indicative of backwardness in everything else. "Hurray for those who never invented anything," defiantly wrote Aimé Césaire, the Martinique poet of African ancestry who is one of the great contemporary spokesmen for the cultural movement called *négritude*.

But Césaire overstated the case. Though far behind Europe in their technical knowledge, Africans are now known to have been skillfully inventive in many ways. They developed tropical farming techniques that have scarcely been bettered to this day. They were good miners and metalworkers, producing, among other things, a steady supply of the gold that went into medieval European currencies, and without which those currencies might well have been impossible. They were astute businessmen, as more than one non-African merchant had occasion to know. They operated political and social systems of considerable flexibility and sophistication. They were superb sculptors.

This complex picture of Africa has been pieced together and interpreted only within the last 20 years by scholars of many kinds. With colonialism going or gone, anthropologists, historians and archeologists have looked into Africa and its popula-

tions far more closely and carefully than ever before. Like the wave of rod-and-gun explorers who a century ago rediscovered the continent's geography, intellectual explorers have rediscovered its history, and have rescued a main section of humanity from unhappy misunderstanding.

It is a history that covers a wide spectrum of belief and thought, action and cooperative enterprise. The high civilizations of the ancient Nile have their place in it—Kush, whose kings and queens challenged Egypt; Axum, a continuous stronghold of Christianity from the Fifth Century. So too do the strong states and empires that flourished beyond the Sahara during Europe's Middle Ages and Renaissance—mysterious Zimbabwe, whose massive stone walls enclosed the temple homes of divine rulers "chosen . . . for their equity"; Kilwa, an island fortress whose trading contacts reached to faraway India and China; Songhai, whose powerful kings encouraged scholarship as well as commerce; Ashanti and Benin, whose sculptors created a religious art of impressive power.

But the record of achievement is not confined to big political systems alone. In the shadow of their pomp and glory rests the modest but impressive achievement of village-level Africa. In community attitudes that joined man to man in a brotherhood of equals, in moral rules that guided social behavior, in beliefs that exalted the spiritual aspects of life above the material, the African village achieved a kind of social harmony that often functioned without any need for centralized authority. This, in fact, was where Africa best displayed its real genius—in its capacity for social organization. It was a talent that operated at village level, and in complex kingdoms. And it operated continuously, throughout a stubborn people's long, lonely and determined effort to tame their vast and inhospitable land. In its own way the epic of Africa ranks with history's other examples of the greatness of man.

DESCRIPTION ET
RECIT HISTORIAL
DV RICHE ROYAVME D'OR DE
GVNEA, aultrement nommé, la coste de l'or de MINA, gisante en certain en-
droict d'Africque: auecq leurs foy, persuasions commerces ou trocs costumes
langaiges, & situations du pais, Villes, Villages, Cabannes, & personnes, ses ports,
haures, & fleuues selon qu'iceulx ont esté recognuz iusques
a ceste heure.

Pareillement vng brieff deduict du passaige que les nauires prennent pour y nauiguer, passant au trauers des Isles de
Canarie, Cabo werde le loing de la Coste de Maniguette iusques au Cap des Trespunctas ou que ladicte
coste commence : en oultre quelque description aussi des riuieres quon visite en singlant de
ladicte Coste, vers le Cap de lopo Consalues, d'ou quon se depart, pour retourner
de pardeca, le tout diligement & exactement descript par l'autheur
qui par diuerses fois y a esté.

P.D.M.

No 9   La magnificence du Roij de Caboislopo gonsalues

A AMSTERDAMME.
Imprime chez Cornille Claesson demourant sur leau au liure d'escripture
Anno M.VIC.V.

AN EARLY ACCOUNT *of the Gold Coast in 1605 shows a king in his pavilion, receiving European travelers.*

TRAVELERS' SPLENDROUS TALES

Ever since stories of lands beyond Egypt began to reach the Greeks in the Fifth Century B.C., Africa has fascinated Europeans. But for centuries so little was known about the continent that every traveler's tale, no matter how fanciful, was eagerly believed. Then, as the Portuguese began their explorations in the 15th Century, accurate information began to filter back. Through accounts such as that of the Dutch traveler Pieter de Marees (*above*), Europeans learned of scholarly centers in the desert, trading cities that rivaled Venice—and black knights who ruled gold-rich empires by force of arms. From such stories it is possible to re-create that world of kingdoms more splendrous than any of the myths.

TIMBUKTU—FABLED CITY OF WISDOM

In the 15th Century, Europeans began to hear travelers' stories about the sophistication and affluence of Timbuktu, the intellectual capital of the Western Sudan. When Benedetto Dei, a Florentine merchant, visited the city in 1470, he confirmed the legends. Dei saw a metropolis, probably much like the one re-created at right, where the streets were crowded with goods borne by caravan from afar. Here the round, windowless huts of the poor lay in the shadows of ornate mosques and the many-windowed homes of the rich. The earliest full account of Timbuktu to appear in Europe came from the traveler-historian Leo Africanus, a Moor who in the 16th Century described the city's resplendent court life, and its scholars, "bountifully maintained at the king's cost."

Tales of the city's university, of its stone palace and busy markets, tantalized the imagination of Europeans—until 1828, when a French adventurer made a pilgrimage to Timbuktu. He found that countless raids by neighboring tribesmen had reduced the once-splendid metropolis to a "mass of ill-looking houses built of earth."

AN AUDIENCE
WITH THE KING OF MALI

The kingdom of Mali, which included Timbuktu, was in the 14th Century the wealthiest and most powerful nation in the Western Sudan. Its court ceremony dazzled the most sophisticated Arab visitors, who especially admired the royal pomp. When the sultan granted an audience (above) he sat on an ebony throne flanked by elephant tusks and addressed peti-

tioners through his official spokesman, who stood holding a mace at the foot of the steps. To the right of the sultan stood the ominous figure of the executioner, and clustered around the throne were trumpeters and drummers; ordered ranks of courtiers and cavalry commanders sat listening attentively.

Mali's rulers had been converted to Islam in the 11th Century, but the Arab travelers of three centuries later found their religion somewhat altered. The visitors were shocked to discover that many women—even the sultan's daughters—not only were unveiled but appeared stark naked in public. They commended, however, the unusual custom of putting in chains any schoolboy who was slow to memorize the whole Koran.

THE BUSTLING PORT OF KILWA

From the 12th to 15th Centuries, the chief trading center in East Africa—and one of the liveliest in the entire world—was the prosperous island city of Kilwa. Located off the coast of Tanganyika, Kilwa received goods from the interior and exchanged them for products of foreign lands. On any given day along the shoreline *(left)* workers could be seen loading their masters' dhows with African gold, iron, ivory and coconuts, and unloading textiles and jewelry from India and exquisite porcelain from China. Kilwa's culture became so international and well established that about 1500, when Portuguese traders first arrived in their caravels *(upper left)*, the only notable contributions they made were a few food crops such as avocados and cashews, and a few new words that were incorporated into the native Swahili—words for such refinements as "wine" and "snuff."

FIERCE HORSEMEN OF BORNU

Arrayed in armor like medieval European knights, the cavalry-men of Bornu terrorized the central Sudan for more than 200 years, attacking in close formation to the shrill sound of long war trumpets. As early as the 16th Century, Europeans had heard about Bornu's yearly marches against weaker neighbors such as the Bulala people (below). When British explorers

finally entered the kingdom in 1823, they expected to disprove these myths. To their surprise, they discovered that the Negro knights, according to the British report, "were habited in coats of mail composed of iron chain, which covered them from the throat to the knees," and their richly caparisoned horses moved "with great precision and expertness" through intricate maneuvers. Even the greeting given to the British combined a strange kind of knightly courtesy with defiant pride. The horsemen rushed at the Europeans again and again in a series of mock charges, shouting "Welcome!"—a gesture, wrote the explorers, which gave "the compliment . . . very much the appearance of a declaration of contempt for [our] weakness."

2
CIVILIZATIONS OF THE NILE

The majesty of ancient Egypt dazzled all the peoples who came within its radiance. Even the Greeks, who saw the country only in its far decline, had no difficulty in recognizing its greatness and accepting it as, in more ways than one, the mother of their own civilization. With a few exceptions, wrote the Greek historian Herodotus in the Fifth Century B.C., "the names of all the gods have been known in Egypt from the beginning of time." This venerable age and eminence tended to separate Egypt in men's minds from the rest of Africa. What could the peoples within the African continent have to do with the brilliant civilization that had guided all the early enterprise of the Mediterranean?

Herodotus, as it turns out, already had the answer. It must be "clear to any intelligent observer," he said, "that the Egypt to which we sail nowadays is, as it were, the gift of the river and has come only recently into the possession of its inhabitants." Allowing for the cool exaggeration of "only recently," he was right. The central fact about Egypt's origins was that even if many of its political and social ideas were taken from its Near Eastern neighbors, its culture was basically African. And this culture was inseparably linked to the Stone Age peoples who populated the green Sahara during the long epoch of its fertility.

Habitable land first began to appear in the lower valley and Delta of the Nile probably about 10,000 years ago. Before that the river was immensely wide, bordered by marshland and swamps. As dry ground emerged from the dwindling waters, settlers pressed into it from the grasslands to the west. In the next few millennia they learned to grow annual crops and use a simple sort of plow. What these early Egyptians looked like, no one knows, but they doubtlessly preserved certain characteristics of the peoples of the Sahara.

Shortly after 3400 B.C. two small kingdoms emerged, one along the upper reaches of the Nile, the other along the silted meadows of the Delta. Some scholars believe that this advanced political life was the fruit of migrant leadership from the Near East. Others argue that it was entirely a local development, that the Nile farmers themselves, with their growing wealth and complexity of life, needed and so evolved a more embracing kind of

COLUMNS AT MUSAWWARAT, *amid ruined structures built 2,000 years ago, give mute evidence of the advanced architecture of the kingdom of Kush. The undecipherability of Kush script shrouds this great nation in mystery.*

rule. However it arose, this new civilization at once took a direction manifestly different from its contemporaries in lands to the east. Egyptian habits of thought and behavior were, from the beginning, special to Egypt.

Some three centuries later these two kingdoms were united under a ruler whom the records generally call Menes, and it was with Menes that the long line of Egyptian dynasties began. No more than 600 years later the mighty rulers of the Fourth Dynasty built the pyramids at Gizeh. It is as though the whole majestic structure of Egyptian civilization grew from infancy to ripeness across a few centuries. And yet, in many remarkable ways that are amply documented by art objects and fragmentary inscriptions, the early kingdoms were the parents of all that followed. The motives and means that made possible the remarkable achievement of the pyramids—the religious belief, political power, mathematical skill and mobilization of labor—had already taken shape in predynastic times.

But if Egypt owed a debt to its African past, it also repaid the debt. Many old beliefs and institutions in the rest of Africa seem to echo those of Egypt. The spiritual power, or "godship," of the pharaohs had parallels in the "divine kingship" of later, lesser rulers far to the south of the swamps, deserts and forests that separated Egypt from the African interior. In many parts of western Africa people apparently held the ram to be a symbol of divinity, just as the Egyptians did. And until modern times men and women of the Congo, thousands of miles from the Nile, rested their heads on wooden pillows of a style and shape remarkably like those of Egypt.

It would be simplest to say that these things merely indicate a slow, if indirect, penetration of Egyptian ideas and habits into the heart of the continent. But the truth is more complex. Some of the similarities point back to the time of the Stone

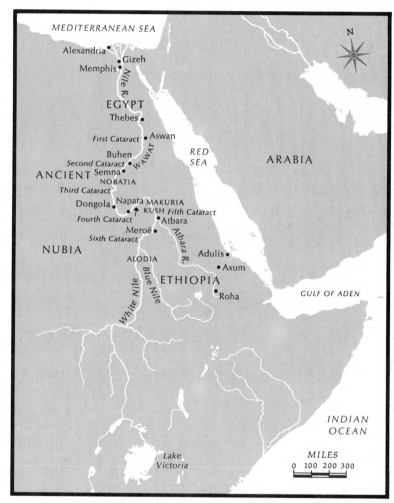

THE LANDS OF THE NILE *were a seedbed of African cultures from 3400 B.C. to 1500 A.D. The influence of civilizations that grew along the river, centered in cities like Thebes, Napata and Meroë, was felt to the far reaches of the continent.*

Age "nursery" cultures in the old Sahara. Just as so much of Egyptian culture came out of this land, so it seems likely that the tides of influence also flowed the other way: Egyptian Africans carried their new culture back to their Saharan African brothers. Thus the inner African "echoes of Egypt" show the land of the Nile to be not only a geographical part of the mother continent but an integral part of its cultural structure as well.

With the passage of time this cultural interpenetration deepened and took new directions. As Egypt grew stronger, pharaohs sent military and commercial expeditions southward, as well as westward. There are written records of journeys by ship to the "land of Punt" at the southern end of the Red Sea in the time of the Fourth Dynasty (2613 to 2494 B.C.), and other records tell of land caravans into the unknown countries of the far southwest in the Sixth Dynasty, about 150 years later. Westward the Egyptians clashed repeatedly with the nomads of the Libyan grasslands, but they also traded with these Saharan peoples. Rock paintings in the Sahara show Egyptian boats, and it is possible that these boats plied Saharan rivers as late as 2000 B.C.

It was toward the south, however, that later Egyptian influence was most persistent and most enduring. The pharaohs thrust their frontiers beyond the First Cataract of the Nile about 2000 B.C., and built great forts at strategic narrows like Buhen and Semna. Gradually they penetrated and conquered the Nubian lands that lay beyond. Then in the 18th Dynasty two Pharaohs with imperial ambitions, Amenophis I and Thutmose I, pushed their conquests even farther. Thutmose sent his armies up the unbroken stretch of water that lies between the Third and Fourth Cataracts, generally known as the Dongola Reach, and established forts and colonies to the south, bringing the lands of Irtet, Wawat and Kush under an Egyptian control that would continue unbroken for 500 years.

But these conquered peoples, though deeply influenced by Egyptian beliefs and techniques, were never more than partially assimilated into Egyptian civilization. They continued to hold onto their own traditions and retained their cultural identity. Later, when Egypt's fortunes waned, the subject nations saw a chance to triumph over their former conquerors and boldly seized it, leaving Egypt with little power south of the Buhen narrows. Then it was that the Kushites, living in the region that is now the Sudan, set upon a memorable enterprise. They built the greatest of the old civilizations of inner Africa.

Spanning 1,000 years, the Kushite civilization was notable both for its profound indebtedness to Egypt and for the persistence of its non-Egyptian identity. Its history falls into two main periods. It was founded just prior to 750 B.C. by princes who made their capital at Napata, near the southern end of the Dongola Reach. Napata remained its center for some 200 years, during which time many aspects of Kushite culture continued to be colored by the ideas of its Egyptian neighbors—not least, the worship of the god Amon. Then the capital was shifted south to Meroë, much farther into the Sudan, and a new Kushite civilization came into existence, at once more brilliant and more coherent than its predecessor.

Before this happened, however, Napatan Kush turned itself briefly into a great military power. Reversing the trend of 1,000 years, it attacked Egypt. Napatan kings led their armies northward. "Forward against it! Mount the walls! Penetrate the houses!" run the exhortations in one of their conquering inscriptions, in this case marking King Piankhy's assault on Memphis, which "was taken as (by) a flood of water." Piankhy's father had begun this conquest with the seizure of Thebes and most of Upper Egypt in the first half of the

Eighth Century B.C. Piankhy added Memphis and much of Lower Egypt between 751 and 730 B.C. And Piankhy's brother Shabako brought the fields and towns of the Nile Delta within Kushite power between 707 and 696 B.C.

But the triumph was short-lived. The Kushite King Taharqa, who ruled after Shabako, met an enemy stronger than he was. The Assyrians, raiding down through Israel to the Nile Delta, allied themselves with Egyptian princes and drove out Taharqa and the Kushites. "Five times I hit him with the point of my arrows," boasts an inscription of the Assyrian King Esarhaddon, "and then I laid siege to Memphis, his royal residence: I destroyed, tore down its walls, and burnt it down." Whether or not this was a court scribe's exaggeration, it is a fact that Taharqa retreated south. With the rule of his successor, Tanuatamun, Kushite dominion over Egypt came to a close.

But not Kushite civilization. It was only beginning. After its capital shifted south to Meroë in the Sixth Century B.C., its character changed greatly and flowered. In the riverside pastures near the Sixth Cataract there now appeared fine towns of masonry, and palaces and pyramids which, if less princely than those of Egypt, were nevertheless endowed with a style and dignity of their own. With all this there gradually emerged a civilization of great vigor and importance—although much is still unknown about it.

Meroë had its own alphabetic writing, developed in the late Third or early Second Century B.C., but the language it was used for is not understood, and the script has yet to be deciphered. Other records, by outsiders, are few and inconclusive. Greek writers of classical times occasionally mentioned Kush, calling it Ethiopia (from the Greek word *aithiops*, meaning dark-skinned); the name has confused generations of readers, since modern Ethiopia is unrelated to the Ethiopia of the

Greeks. Not even Herodotus, who saw so much of the world of his time, managed to get to Kush—although he did collect more useful things to say about it than anyone else for over 2,000 years. It is only in the last few decades, with the intensive excavation of the royal tombs, that the story of Kush has begun to emerge. And it was certainly a great story.

It seems likely that Meroë was already an important religious center for the Kushites during the reign of King Aspelta, from 593 to 568 B.C. Its growing domination of its sister city of Napata was probably due to a number of factors. One may have been security. Napata had already suffered one damaging attack from the Egyptian ruler Psammetichus II, and might suffer another. Meroë was less vulnerable. Then, too, as the Sahara got progressively drier, and the desert moved closer to the Nile, the royal cattle may have overgrazed the region around Napata. But two other developments offer even more persuasive reasons for Meroë's ascendancy. One was the introduction of iron into the Kushite way of life; the other was the rise among the Kushite people of what today would be called a sense of nationhood.

When the Assyrians "came down like a wolf on the fold," driving the Kushite kings out of Lower Egypt, they had the advantage of iron weapons. The Egyptians, and to some extent the Kushites, too, had long known the use of iron but had barely begun to explore it. Set in their ways by countless centuries of habit and self-confidence, the Nile peoples saw no reason to change from their customary copper and bronze. But iron weapons were harder, and it was also easier to make a large number of them once the techniques of working the metal were understood. One of the great consequences of the Assyrian invasion of the Nile Valley, perhaps the greatest, was the introduction of iron into general use for tools and weapons.

The Kushites, adopting this new technology, found the region around Napata poor in iron ore, while Meroë was relatively rich in it. Meroë may also have had more trees, and hence more smelting fuel. In the centuries that followed, the new capital grew into a great ironworking center—tall heaps of ironworking waste may still be seen there—and was probably the source from which iron technology spread southward, into the heart of the continent. One British archeologist was so convinced of this that he called Meroë "the Birmingham" of ancient Africa.

But industry was not the only reason for the shift from Napata to Meroë. The move was accompanied, or at least closely followed, by a growing sense of national identity. Although much that came from Egypt continued to remain a part of Kushite daily life, there was a steady movement toward purely local beliefs and ideas. Beginning with the reign of King Nastasen, 328 to 308 B.C., Meroitic civilization increasingly acquired an accent that was wholly its own. Meroitic hieroglyphs came into use, followed by a Meroitic alphabet and script. Meroitic gods and forms of worship were substituted for Egyptian ones. New and original styles appeared in architecture, pottery and much else besides. The few traces of Egyptian culture that remained, notably in royal ceremonials and in the use of Egyptian hieroglyphs on royal tombs, lingered for much the same reasons that Latin did in Western society.

By the reign of Ergamenes, who ruled from 225 to 200 B.C., the Egyptian ram god's position as the supreme deity was being challenged by a lion god, never seen before, and often shown with three faces and four arms. Similarly the Kushites raised another African beast, the elephant, to a position of great importance. Like the Carthaginians during the same period, the Kushites used elephants for warfare and royal prestige. It is even possible that one of the largest known Kushite buildings, a massive affair of walls and ramps near a place called Musawwarat, was a stable and enclosure for the royal elephants; there are several elegant portraits of these creatures in its masonry.

But the outstanding attribute of these Kushite peoples was not their originality in devising new gods or domesticating elephants. Rather, it was their enterprise and eminence in trade. Separated by seas of sand and barren rock from much of the rest of the world, they learned to stand on their own feet and improve their lot through anything that the old world of the upper Nile could offer. Much about them, in this respect, suggests the ancient Greeks: they were impatient of tradition, eager for any new thing.

Certainly they traveled a great deal, and in many directions. They traded northward with Egypt, and had their own ports on the Red Sea, through which they shared in the trade with Arabia, East Africa, India and perhaps even China. They pushed up the White Nile to the borders of modern Uganda, and hints of their presence, or at least of their influence, have been found as far west as the region of Lake Chad. Wherever they went they brought back new things and new ideas, adding them to their own stock or transforming them to their own use. Even though the systematic excavation of the cities of Kush has only just begun, the evidence of the range of their journeyings and borrowings is extraordinary. Greek civilization is represented by a fine bronze head of Dionysus, sculpted in Alexandria. Roman influence is reflected by the architecture of at least one of the pillared temples at the ancient city of Naga. And Kush's many-armed lion god is strangely reminiscent of India's Hindu god Shiva.

Furthermore, the Kushites apparently traveled sometimes for reasons other than trade. In the First Century B.C., after Rome had conquered

Egypt, Kush sent ambassadors to Rome (and once the Emperor Nero sent two Roman centurions to Kush—to see if it was worth adding to the Empire). Then, in the First Century A.D., some time after the Crucifixion, an official of the Queen of Kush (the Bible, using the Greek word, calls her the Queen of Ethiopia) met the apostle Philip on "the road that goeth down from Jerusalem to Gaza," who "preached unto him Jesus." Three centuries later a Greek writer named Heliodorus left a memorial of another kind. He composed a romantic epic about a Kushite princess who is carried off to Greece and marries a Greek nobleman.

Yet Meroitic civilization, for all its contacts with the world and its physical accomplishments, suffered an almost total eclipse. Not even its reputation survived the ravages of time. The decline set in about 200 A.D., when its vital trade routes north and east were obstructed by new rivals and enemies, hungry nomads from the scorching deserts on either side of the Nile. These nomads infiltrated the Meroitic homelands, and by the year 300 Meroitic power was all but gone. In 320 the last King

of Kush, the 72nd ruler of his line, was laid to rest in a tiny pyramid of brick; his name was apparently Malequerebar.

Several years after Malequerebar's death the nomad infiltrators of Kush were themselves attacked. Their assailant was a king of Ethiopia, in this case the real Ethiopia. His name was Ezana, and he left behind for posterity in his capital at Axum an inscription of unique value, describing his invasion. The nomads (Ezana calls them the Red Noba and Black Noba) were interfering with Ezana's deputies and messengers, and fighting among themselves in violation of their promise: "Twice and thrice they had broken their solemn oath. . . ." He decided to teach them a lesson. Marching north with his armies in 330, he scattered the Noba "at the ford of Kemalke" on the river Takaze, and then followed them hard for 23 days until he reached "the towns of masonry" of the Kushites. He seized and pillaged these, along with the Noban "towns of straw." Another inscription says that Ezana returned from Kush with a booty of 3,112 head of cattle and 6,224 sheep—a vast parade of livestock

ROYAL ELEPHANTS *hold the ropes of a group of war captives in this stone frieze in the Lion Temple at Musawwarat, thought to have been built by the Kushite King Sherakarer in the First Century A.D. The Kushites, who conquered Egypt in the Eighth Century B.C., domesticated elephants for use in war and paraded them at royal events.*

that arrived in Ethiopia engulfed in a cloud of dust.

After this, little was heard of Meroitic Kush until some 1,400 years later, when a Scottish traveler, James Bruce, sighted some of its ruins and wrote about them in a book—which his 18th Century readers generally disbelieved. But Meroitic civilization did not, of course, simply disappear. Part of it, at least, was taken over by the immigrant Noba. Acquiring a taste for urban life, they abandoned their rural huts and settled in the remains of the fine masonry towns of Kush. They adopted a number of Meroitic customs and crafts (though not, unfortunately, the art of writing) and built a minor civilization of their own. Archeologists have called this superficial culture by the cautious name of X-Group. It flourished mainly in the northern towns of Kush, and its history seems to have been largely one of small wars between petty chiefs. And yet this X-Group—part Noban, part Meroitic—produced a memorable by-product, for out of it in the Sixth Century emerged the glories of Christian Nubia.

Though most of their written records are lost,

the three Christian kingdoms of ancient Nubia—Nobatia in the north, Makuria in the middle and Alodia in the south—have left behind some proofs of their achievements. The most splendid of these are a few superb murals, discovered only a few years ago and rescued from the rising waters of Egypt's new Aswan Dam. They were at a place called Faras, and they were unearthed by a Polish archeological expedition, in response to an appeal from the Sudanese government for emergency archeological research in the lands to be covered by the dam. Probing into the ruins of large religious buildings, pulling away sand from aisles and chapels, the archeologists came upon the murals, still glowing in their original colors, and cut them out for preservation in Warsaw and Khartoum.

The kingdoms of Christian Nubia arose mainly through the missionary enterprise of monks from Constantinople, and especially through one monk, Julian, who arrived in the region of the old Kushite kingdom in 543. The story of Julian's ministry among the Nubians has been told with a wealth of detail by another monk, John of Ephesus, who had

O GOD, HAVE MERCY
ON THE SOUL OF BROTHER
PHILOTHEOS, THE FATHER
OF THE REFECTORY.

been sent by the Roman Emperor Justinian around the same time on a similar mission: to convert the Ethiopians. One of the chief difficulties Julian faced seems to have been the heat. According to John, Julian "used to say that from nine o'clock until four in the afternoon he was obliged to take refuge in caves full of water, where he sat undressed except for a linen garment such as people in the country wear."

A century after Julian's arrival, Egypt was overrun by Muslim Arabs, and Nubia was all but cut off from the rest of the Christian world. For 600 years its kings and bishops, contemporaries of the kings and bishops building the Holy Roman Empire in Europe, were practically unknown to that Empire, and had only themselves to rely on for faith and reassurance. To the north lay Muslim Egypt, and although relations between the two nations were not bad—Nubia was even accustomed to thinking of southern Egypt as belonging within

its own sphere of influence, since it had once belonged to the old kingdom of Kush—it was the proximity of Egypt that eventually brought on the Nubian kingdoms' downfall.

Egypt under its Fatimid rulers accepted the Nubian Christians under sufferance, just as it accepted the Coptic Christians within its own borders. But in the 12th Century the Fatimids were ousted by the Saracens, Muslims of a more militant cast, who invaded Egypt from Syria under their powerful leader Saladin. Already at war with the crusading Christian knights of western Europe, the Saracen rulers of Egypt soon moved south to deal with the Christians nearer home. In 1276 they placed their own nominee on the throne of Nobatia, the most northerly of the Nubian kingdoms. Makuria, the middle kingdom, held out for another century, and Alodia, southernmost of the Christian trio, was not engulfed by Islam until the 15th Century. Nine hundred years after the earliest missionaries had

reached the homeland of the vanished empire of Meroë, Christian times were over there.

Far away, at the other end of the Red Sea, however, another branch of African Christianity lived on undefeated. Ethiopia, whose King Ezana had put down the Red and Black Noba in the Fourth Century, had become officially Christian with Ezana's conversion. But its legendary contact with Christianity was rooted much further back in time, in the Biblical story of the Queen of Sheba, who went up from Ethiopia to King Solomon's Jerusalem "with a very great train, with camels that bear spices, and very much gold and precious stones." King Solomon fell in love with her, and gave her a son. That son, Menelik, became a famous Ethiopian ruler and founded the line of the Lion of Judah, from whom the current ruler, the Emperor Haile Selassie, claims to be descended.

Thus goes the legend. Ethiopia's factual history is a good deal less romantic and a good deal more complicated. Some 500 years before the birth of Christ, there emerged on the southwest flank of the Red Sea a number of settlements whose culture was largely influenced by the Sabaeans, a people of southern Arabia. They were trading folk who worshiped Almaqah, a Sabaean moon god, and they wrote in a fine script. Gradually they merged with the local peoples to form a new culture which —as often happens with merged cultures—developed a dynamism all its own.

Like their Kushite contemporaries at Meroë, these early Ethiopians were an enterprising lot. They welcomed merchants from Greek-ruled Egypt, and their principal port, Adulis, soon became a major point of interchange for goods from the Mediterranean, Arabia and the eastern lands of the Indian Ocean. Their trading contacts extended far down the African coast, and they made expeditions into the inner African lands. By the Second Century A.D. they had built a strong state behind the coastal

41

hills, with a capital at Axum. It was from Axum that King Ezana rode north to punish the Noba.

Axum remained the chief power in the region washed by the southern Red Sea until the Eighth Century, leaving behind as monuments to its majesty tall needles of masonry and finely wrought gold coins. Merchants of Axum and Adulis, wrote an Alexandrian merchant in about 523, traded as far as Ceylon and sold their ivory in Persia, Arabia, India and Byzantium. Their merchant vessels were so famous that a Mesopotamian poet used them to describe the progress of a royal caravan: it forged ahead, he said, like one of the ships of Adulis, whose "prow cuts through the foam of the water as a gambler divides the dust with his hand." In 531 the same Julian who ministered to the Nubians was sent by the Emperor Justinian to the Axumite court. He reported that the King received him dressed in a linen garment embroidered with gold and set with pearls, and that the royal throne was a gilded chariot drawn by four elephants; flutes played during his audience.

Greek was still officially the language of this court, but Sixth Century Axum was in the process of acquiring a literary language of its own, Geez. The New Testament had already been translated into it—probably by a group of Syrian monks, since the text was based not on the Bible used in Alexandria, but on the one used in Antioch, in Syria.

With the rise of Islam the history of the Axumite empire becomes obscure. Cut off from the rest of the Christian world even more completely than the Nubians to the north, the Ethiopians struggled to survive against Muslims and marauding pagan neighbors. For a long time nothing was heard but a confused and distant clash of arms. When the world at large took note of Axum again, it had been transformed. Its spiritual loyalties were still vibrantly Christian, but it was now a Christianity deep-rooted in the Ethiopian soil. In the 12th Century one of its most famous kings, Lalibela, presided over the construction of some of the most unusual religious structures in the world—a series of 10 chapels and churches, dark-aisled and pillared, hewn out of the living rock in the mountains of Lasta near his capital of Roha.

This was the Ethiopia that the Portuguese discovered in the 15th Century in their quest for the legendary Prester John, who supposedly ruled over a Christian kingdom in the heart of Africa. It was an Ethiopia very like the kingdoms of medieval Europe, a land ruled by proud and contumacious nobles bound in fealty to their king, with a hierarchy of lesser nobles and vassals below them and, at the bottom, landless peasants laboring for all. For a while relations between the two Christian kingdoms were friendly. Portugal sent a military expedition under the son of Vasco da Gama to help Ethiopia against the Muslims; Ethiopia welcomed Portuguese missionaries.

But the friendship did not last. Portugal's missionaries were loyal to Rome; Ethiopia was loyal to the Coptic bishops in Alexandria and refused to change. It was loyal to other old ways, too. "In this feudal country," wrote two French travelers, the brothers D'Abbadie, in the 1830s, "men are united by an infinity of ties which would count for nothing in Europe. They live together in reciprocal dependence and solidarity which they value highly and consider a matter of pride, and which influence all they do." A man with no fixed obligation to his society was "in their eyes outside the social order." The D'Abbadies had discovered something in feudal Ethiopia that was true of all African societies: morality was determined by social service; each man had a moral duty to serve the group. This sense of identity with the social group lay at the root not only of complex societies like Ethiopia, but of primitive societies that had no apparent structure at all.

OVERHANGING ROCKS *shelter many of the 15,000 rock paintings in the Sahara's high central plateaus—the world's greatest gallery of prehistoric art.*

THE OLDEST AFRICANS

Eight thousand years ago, while vestiges of the Ice Age chilled Europe, the Sahara we know today as an empty, arid desert was a fertile region whose flowing rivers and grassy valleys teemed with fish and wild animals. During the next 6,000 years in this inviting land, waves of migrants developed a series of increasingly advanced societies, which they recorded in a collection of remarkably beautiful scenes carved and painted on native rock—the most complete record of early African civilizations and of Stone Age life to be found anywhere.

Around 2000 B.C.—because of a diminishing flow of airborne moisture from southern Europe or some other climatic change—the Sahara started drying up. Animals and humans began to disperse, but the paintings—protected by dry air and nests of pit vipers—remained. In 1956 a French explorer-ethnologist, Henri Lhote, began an intensive study of the neglected frescoes at Tassili n'Ajjer, a forbidding plateau 900 miles southeast of Algiers. Faithfully copying 800 of the paintings, Lhote and a team of artists emerged after 16 months with an intriguing portrait of a once-green Sahara, and of Africa's cultural beginnings.

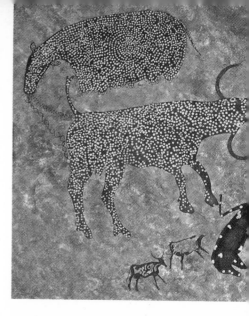

SPOTTED OXEN *(right) were wild when these were drawn about 4000 B.C. But within a few years, cattle were pasturing on Saharan grasslands in domesticated herds.*

LOPING HARES *were pictured about 4500 B.C. Lhote's group discovered this fresco in a sheltered spot, painted directly on the stone; portraits in exposed areas were often incised into the rock for greater permanence.*

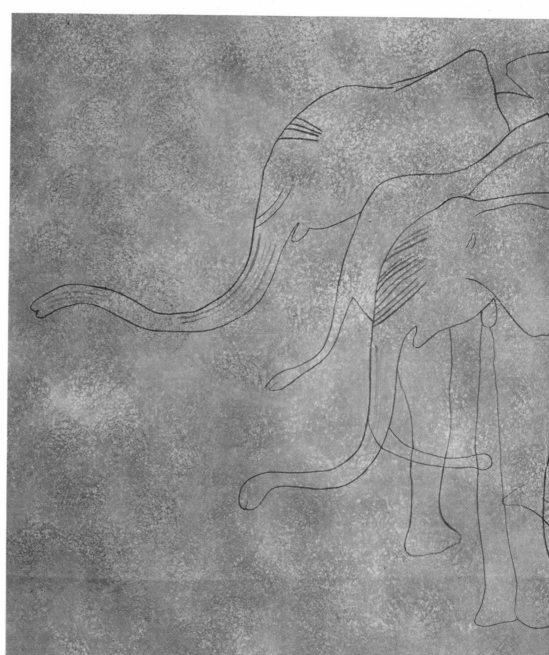

PEACEFUL ELEPHANTS *are shown in an unusually graceful drawing done during a period when the cave artists attained a style of great simplicity and sophistication. By 1000 B.C. elephants had departed from the dry Sahara.*

WILDLIFE OF A GREEN SAHARA

Eroded by wind and water into steep, many-sided gorges and gulleys, the Tassili plateau was an ideal working place for the primitive artists. On the protected stone walls of niches and shelters they drew what they saw around them. Occasionally they pictured sights seen on journeys east into Egypt and north to Libya, but mostly they portrayed animals. Among these portraits are outsized pictures of rhinoceroses 25 feet long and elephants 15 feet tall—the largest prehistoric drawings known. In some scenes these elephants are gathered placidly around pools; in others, giraffes nibble the cypresses and alders that dot the land, and gazelles and ostriches bound through verdant valleys. Through painstaking analysis of hundreds of pictures such as these, scholar Lhote and his small task force of artist-researchers came to the surprising conclusions on which the text and captions in this essay are based.

SPINDLY GIRAFFES *show up in many Tassili paintings, from the most ancient to the most recent. The animal, hunted for both its flesh and its pliable hide, probably disappeared from the Sahara in the First Century A.D.*

A CRUDE CAMEL, *ridden by a warrior, has a type of harness still in local use. Drawn centuries later than the other animals pictured here, it reflects a decline in Saharan art that coincided with the region's decline into desert.*

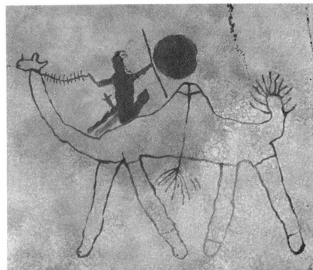

SCENES FROM A SHADOWY PAST

The rock paintings of the Tassili picture the comings and goings of many peoples and animals. Some scholars have classified them roughly into four periods, naming each after its dominant figure: the Hunter (6000 to 4000 B.C.), the Herder (4000 to 1500 B.C.), the Horse (1500 to 600 B.C.) and the Camel (from about 600 B.C. on).

The Hunter, the man of the middle Stone Age, was an arrant individualist who walked about with throwing sticks, clubs and spears, and lived by killing wild animals. Though he could make knives, needles and fishhooks out of stone and bone, his social organization remained primitive. The Herder of the late Stone Age, however, practiced simple hoe agriculture and domesticated cattle, goats and sheep. The Herders' rock paintings, the most skillfully executed of the Tassili collection, show man as a social being—engaging in rituals (right), looking after his herds, doing domestic chores.

This pleasant pastoral period, however, actually marked the beginning of the end. As the centuries wore on, the Sahara began to desiccate; by the time domesticated horses were brought in from Egypt, about 1500 B.C., most of the wild animals were gone. But the horse could not survive permanently in the harshening climate. It was time for a species better suited to the conditions. Before the Christian era began, the camel came into its own as a mount and beast of burden. By then the Sahara had become essentially the desert it is today.

RITUAL SACRIFICE *may be the fate of the unwilling sheep seen at right, which is being separated from its brethren and led off by white-robed herdsmen in this Tassili painting of about 3000 B.C.*

CEREMONIAL FIGURES, *some painted white, participate in what may be a tri*

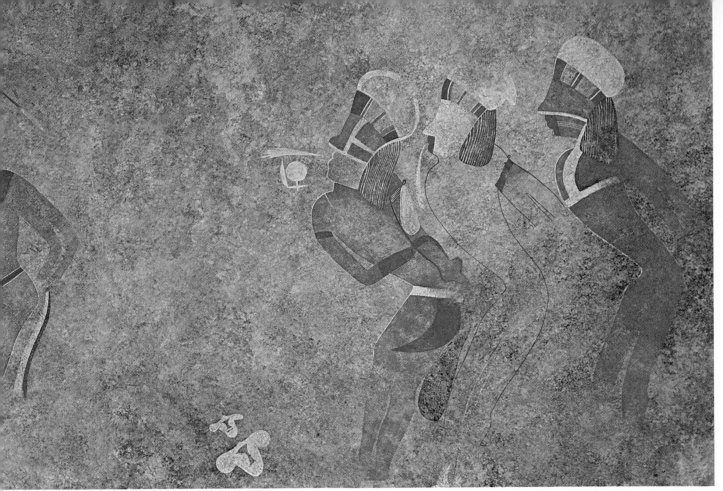

...tiation drawn about 4000 B.C. The men wear striped, rounded headdresses with a faintly Egyptian look; the women wear simple caps and narrow loincloths.

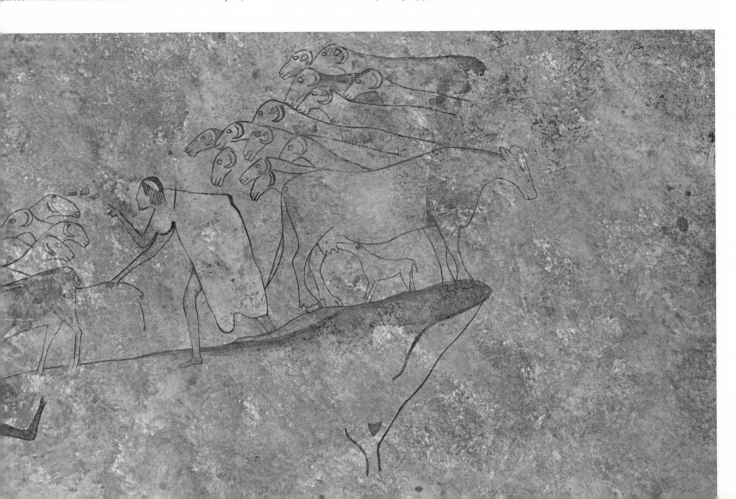

A DOMESTIC SCENE *shows cattle gathered next to a group of huts represented by stylized white ovals. Behind a line of calves tethered to a rope, women and children busy themselves with chores.*

THE HERDSMEN'S TRANQUIL LIFE

Saharan civilization reached its peak during the 2,500 years of the Herder period. Cattle grazed across the savanna, tended by men carrying bows and arrows and accompanied by dogs. The hunting of wild animals still went on, but cattle were now all-important. Artists lavished great care in rendering the beasts; mottled hides, delicate hoofs and swishing tails were handsomely depicted, and special attention was paid to horns—short and long, thick and thin, crescent and lyre-shaped. These valued animals made possible a more settled and civilized life than in the day of the hunter. The herders began to build huts of wickerwork and dried grasses, clustered into villages. Paintings of the period show scenes of domesticity and relative plenty—women standing before their cooking pots, men with axes in hand preparing to split wood, children lying under coverlets, people sitting in circles and talking, women harvesting in the fields.

DRAWING WATER *about 1000 B.C., two men work with the same sort of leather bucket still used by Saharan nomads. An ox is drinking from a trough.*

GRACEFUL WOMEN, *their arms and legs extended as in a curiously beautiful ballet, Lhote believes are actually gathering grain (represented by dots). It is probably wild grain; there is no evidence that the Stone Age Saharan peoples had cultivated cereal crops.*

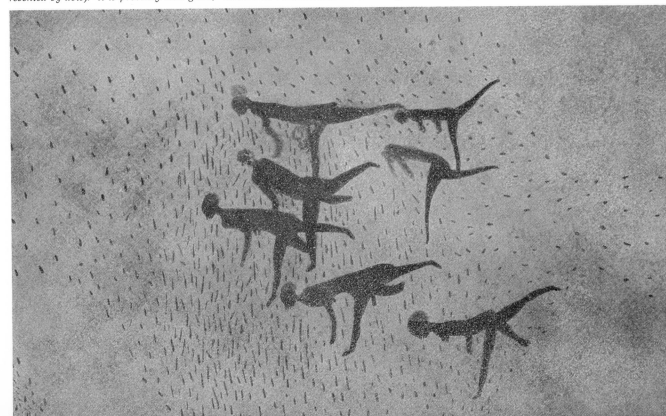

MAKING MUSIC, *one man strums a stringed instrument while another holds a long, stick-like object, possibly a kind of flute. Both musicians are wearing feathers on their heads.*

DANCING IN PROCESSION *(below), men wear decorative, flared leggings and what appear to be masks. Women are shown with rounded stomachs and long, ribbonlike headdresses.*

LIVELY SCENES OF MUSIC AND DANCE

The peace and plenty of the Sahara's pastoral era are reflected not only in the skill of the paintings of that period, but also in other arts such as music and dancing shown in the paintings. Both men and women took part in dances *(below)* that must have had some religious significance.

To record pictures such as these, Henri Lhote and his artists first had to sponge off the dust-covered frescoes and bring out their color with precious water carried in on camels. Then, frequently standing on tiptoe or lying on their backs in niches, they traced precise copies of the wall images, matching the subtle colors afterward. Only then were the results rendered in permanent gouache and oils.

THE BUSY, ELEGANT WOMEN OF THE SAHARA

Women played a surprisingly active role in early Saharan life compared to the veiled ladies of later North African eras. Apparently there was a strict division of labor between the men and the women. Many of the Tassili frescoes show women tending cattle, raising children, gathering and preparing food. The men hunted with bows and arrows and fashioned implements out of stone. Women also made baskets, pottery, bracelets, necklaces, awls and other objects for household and personal use.

Perhaps the most striking aspect of these Saharan wives and mothers, however, is the elegance and care with which many of them are represented. The two paintings shown here, one of a brown-skinned woman and the other of four lighter ladies, are quite different in content and artistic style. Yet both endow their subjects with dignity, indicating the regard in which women were held.

A SEATED MOTHER *(left) tends her baby on a rug made of an animal skin. Her hair style, of small, tightly coiled braids, resembles that of some West African women of today.*

WOMEN RIDERS *mounted on horned oxen wear capes and hairdos astonishingly modern in style. They are part of a scene which shows a whole community moving to another camp.*

ARMED HERDSMEN, *dressed in long yellow cloaks and carrying bows, advance into combat. The long-robed figure at top, wielding a trumpet or a throwing club, is probably their commander. At the left, other strange, cloaked figures move in to parley or fight.*

A WEARY WARRIOR, *returning to camp, collapses from exhaustion or wounds as two figures move toward him in an attempt to help. The woman, at left, holds what appears to be a digging stick, still used for tilling the soil and unearthing edible roots.*

FIERCE BATTLES WITH NEW INVADERS

As the Saharans' societies developed, war appeared more and more frequently in paintings of their everyday lives. During pastoral times they were sometimes depicted in battle array, perhaps to settle the rights to a disputed herd. But if war was an occasional necessity for the herdsmen, it was a passion with the horsemen who appeared in the last millennium before Christ. According to one theory, these warriors rolled in from the north behind steeds harnessed to war chariots, pitting their javelins and round shields against the herders' bows. The Greek historian Herodotus indicates that the invaders may have been the Garamantes, a Berber-speaking North African people. Caught between the Sahara's fierce new invaders and its worsening climate, the peaceful herdsmen gradually disappeared.

MYSTERIES OF LAW AND LIFE

The Saharans painted on virtually every suitable rock face in the Tassili, often drawing new pictures over old; in one place Henri Lhote found as many as 16 superimposed scenes. The paintings leave no doubt that some of these societies were highly organized. But aspects of their organization and operation remain the subject of educated guesses. Lhote believes that the painting at right, for example, shows the workings of justice. The man at the center, found guilty of some crime, is being led off by an official in a striped hat. At left are two other officials, one of whom may be the jailer or executioner. A group of robed justices, their work completed, hurries off at lower right.

Other scholars have advanced different hypotheses for this and other mysterious tableaux that may represent aspects of primitive institutions. Anthropologists believe that the early Sahara was a "nursery" for cultures that spread through the continent. How much Africa's kingdoms owe these cultures may never be fully known.

3

THE TRADITION
OF THE TRIBE

ASHANTI BLACKSMITHS *forge tools in a village hut in Ghana. Because of their ability to produce iron implements and weapons from crude ore, blacksmiths for centuries have held respected positions in African tribes.*

"No one following an elephant needs to knock the dew off the grass," says an old Ashanti proverb. And no one looking at the ruins of ancient Egypt needs to be told that once a great civilization passed that way. But most of the 19th Century Europeans who penetrated Africa south of the Sahara found it hard to believe that the inner continent could have known any sort of history at all. Here were no monuments to a past majesty, and certainly no peoples who could be connected even remotely with some former greatness. No trail of history appeared to lead through the apparent primeval simplicity.

Consequently the first Europeans who thrust their way northward from South Africa a century ago made a discovery that astonished them. Fording the sluggish Limpopo River and ascending the uplands of southern Rhodesia, they came upon a group of stone ruins, some of them surrounded by walls as much as 32 feet high. Clearly they were the remnants of an unknown civic power. "We climbed onto the wall and walked along this until we reached the conical tower," wrote one of these early explorers, Willi Posselt. "The interior was covered with dense bush: tall trees towered above the undergrowth, and suspended from them were masses of 'monkey rope' by means of which we lowered ourselves and entered the ruins. . . . Profound silence brooded over the scene."

Posselt was describing the Great Temple at Zimbabwe, seat of a flourishing African empire that had declined only a century before. The kings of Zimbabwe had controlled an area that included much of what is now Rhodesia and central Mozambique, and had grown rich and powerful on gold. Under the rule of one of their dynasties, Zimbabwe's originally simple buildings had been transformed into the imposing royal enclosure which Posselt had come upon. But of this Posselt knew nothing, nor would he probably have believed it. Although his African bearers, on nearing Zimbabwe, "sat down and solemnly saluted by clapping their hands," as though following some time-honored ritual, he never imagined them to have any connection with the ruins. To him, and to most of his contemporaries, Africans were simple folk, living in smoke-filled mud huts, possessing nothing but their spears, their herds of lean cattle, and a few pots of crude earthenware; Zimbabwe must have been the work of some ingenious and long vanished people from beyond the sea.

In this of course they were simply reflecting the ideas of their time. Nineteenth Century Europeans thought that social order was a steep ladder of racial virtue, with white peoples on the topmost rung and black peoples down at the bottom. "It is a wonderful thing to look at this weird world of human beings—half animal, half children, wholly savage and wholly heathen," wrote the British scholar Henry Drummond, after his visit to East Africa. "It is an education . . . in the meaning and history of man. . . . It is to have watched the dawn of evolution." If occasionally some dissident voice was raised, he was briskly dealt with. Such men were simpletons, said Sir Richard Burton, the noted African traveler; as "everyone who has studied the natural history of man" would agree, Europeans were naturally superior to Africans, and even the Africans knew it.

Working from a wider knowledge and less colorful prejudice, modern Africanists have proved these men to be wrong. Posselt's bearers may indeed have been descended from the very people who built Zimbabwe—the simplicity of African village life is deceptive. Bare and flimsy it may often be, but it is not unchanged since "the dawn of evolution." A century ago, in spite of opinions like Posselt's and Burton's, Africa was already in the broad noontime of a long and fruitful social development. It was a development peculiarly African—more concerned with the amenities of personal relationships than with material progress. Africans, out of necessity, learned to put social harmony and the welfare of the group above all else. These values did not always operate perfectly—what value systems do?— but they were surprisingly consistent. They may still be observed at work today among African peoples who still retain strong links with their past.

The beginnings of this process of social development go back some 2,000 years to the time when Africans emerged from their Stone Age wanderings and settled in communities. As these communal settlements grew in size and became more complex, they called into being a wide variety of systems for regulating society. No doubt many of these systems differed sharply right from the start. But just as probably, many only became different with the passage of time. They varied, for instance, in the size and social relationships of the group; in the means they used to assure peace at home and resolve conflicts with their neighbors; in the methods they adopted for choosing their men of authority and defining their functions. Not least, they varied in the rate at which these means and methods were modified under the pressure of circumstance.

And yet the beliefs and habits of different African peoples also reflected common cultural patterns of thought and action. Many of them held, for instance, that the community consisted of the dead ancestors and the generations still unborn, as well as the living. Many of them observed the same laws about customary matters like land-use, even though they were geographically far apart. And many methods of political organization rested upon kinship patterns that, however different in detail, were essentially the same. African oral history might seldom go back more than 200 years, but African modes of behavior were based on memories that were obviously very old indeed.

Of course, not all of these cultural similarities were uniquely African. Other peoples on other continents have worked out systems of thought and action that are close parallels. Anthropologists like to compare African patterns of social behavior with those of American Indians; historians have found it useful to compare African ideas with those of medieval Europe. Parallels have been noted between King John of England, who was forced to agree in

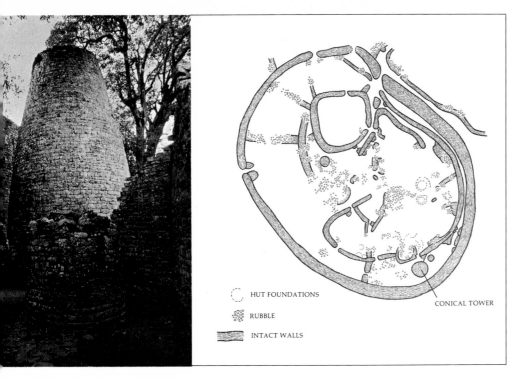

HUT FOUNDATIONS

RUBBLE

INTACT WALLS

CONICAL TOWER

ZIMBABWE'S GREAT TEMPLE, *one of the most spectacular remains of any ancient African civilization, once enclosed within its granite walls a complex of huts, ceremonial shrines, passageways and granaries—now mostly in ruins. Dominating the temple's inner sanctum is a mysterious conical tower of apparently solid masonry (far left), which has baffled treasure seekers and archeologists ever since Zimbabwe was first found by explorers in 1868. Guesses about the tower's function have ranged widely, from a chieftain's gold-filled tomb to a version of a Muslim minaret.*

1215 to let his barons "distress and harass" him if he acted unjustly, and the treatment of unjust kings in a certain East African kingdom. Such a king, wrote the 10th Century Arab historian al-Masudi, "if he depart from the rules of justice," was killed and his heirs debarred from succession.

Nevertheless, for all its points of similarity to other cultures, the African experience grew out of conditions that were peculiar to the African continent. Nothing made this more obvious than the tremendous diversity of the ways in which the continent's peoples worked out the problems of existence. Fighting to survive in the endless plains and dense forests, the swampy valleys and high mountain ranges, each African society devised its own special methods for staying alive and living together. The continent's history is a story with two major themes: one is the restless movement of men and ideas over enormous distances; the other, paradoxically, is the isolation and self-containment of individual communities.

The highlights of this story emerged whenever one group or another embarked on some grand political enterprise that affected its neighbors—and thus entered oral history—or when some learned

traveler like al-Masudi happened to record their exploits. But these highlights by themselves can be misleading. The big and complex African societies only make sense when they are seen against a background of countless small systems that show at close range how the majority of Africans have for centuries met the challenges of life. It is in the minute particulars of these smaller social units that Africa's intrinsic cultural values are revealed.

The simplest African social systems are those which have retained some of the customs of life as it was before the Iron Age began. Tucked away in distant corners, a few peoples still live in these ways. One of them is the pygmies of the Congo rain forests, a retiring folk who have had a varied reputation in the eyes of other men. To the ancient Egyptians, the pygmies were beings of wonder and respect, living somewhere beyond the rim of the southern horizon. Later travelers who glimpsed them were more inclined to regard them as some kind of large monkey.

Not until the present day did the truth about the pygmies become apparent. With the inquiries of the Austrian anthropologist Father Schebesta, and the further research of British anthropologist

THREE DECORATIVE WALLS, *built entirely without mortar, reflect the high level of construction that flourished in what is now Rhodesia. The chevron design at the top is from the ruins at Zimbabwe. The checkered and herringbone patterns below, probably the ruins of a chief's dwelling, were found at Naletale.*

Colin Turnbull, the pygmies finally emerged as human beings and a human society. Far from being animals, they had feelings about their forest world that, in Turnbull's words, "made their life more than just worth living, . . . that made it, with all its hardships and problems and tragedies, a wonderful thing full of joy and happiness and free of care."

Nineteenth Century travelers had put down the pygmies as subhuman because the pygmy life was so bare, so lacking in material sophistication. The same lack baffled and annoyed them in other societies, too. Marching through the lands of the southern Nile in the 1860s, British explorer Samuel Baker looked at the nudely handsome Dinka —living in mud huts, with a few iron spears and fishing hooks for tools—and wrote them off as less noble in character than dogs. They had, he said, none of the attributes of civilization, "neither gratitude, pity, love nor self-denial."

Later travelers among the Dinka and the other peoples of the southern Nile were less contemptuous than Sir Samuel, but still they were puzzled by the apparent absence of any sort of regulatory agency or social order. They found no kings or courts or governments—or none at least that could be traced—and no signs of material progress. The true nature of these Nilotic societies was not understood or seriously studied until the British colonial government, looking for ways to deal with its African subjects, employed anthropologists to search out the "men of authority." Out of these studies, often conducted by scholars of distinction, a body of knowledge has accumulated, revealing a social situation of great complexity.

A Dinka, for example, may wear few clothes, live in a mud and wattle hut, and possess almost nothing of material value, but his life is not haphazard. On the contrary, it is carefully organized, and it revolves around the care of his cattle in the special circumstances of the two great yearly seasons, wet and dry. In July, when the small rains of March give way to drenching storms, and the streams swell into rivers, the Dinka leaves his home in the low-lying plains and drives his herd to high ground. There, on a mound that has been used by his family for generations, and is literally the debris of their campfires, he establishes a *wut*, or cattle camp. In October, when the rainy season ends, he returns home to harvest his crops, but he is again on the move in January, when the dry season sends him toward the river in search of water for his cattle.

The Dinka cattle camp is the nucleus of Dinka society. Each *wut* is surrounded by the *wuts* of other Dinka, all more or less related by complicated bonds of kinship that recognize both matrilineal and patrilineal descent. Each group of *wuts* forms a *gol*, and the sum of all the *gols* in the land of the Dinka is the system under which the Dinka lives. Together they make up a fraternity that, quite literally, governs itself. In this system every person, young or old, married or single, is part of a concerted social action. He is enclosed within a pattern of jobs and duties passed down, usually, through his family. Sons and nephews of the blacksmith succeed him when he dies; sons and nephews of the old priest become the new priests.

Within this ordered society, every occasion has its own convention; little is left to chance. When the Dinka sacrifices a bull or an ox to his gods, he even divides up the carcass according to plan. Its head goes to the village elders, its hump to the sacrificer's immediate family, its shoulder to the middle sons of the wives of the sacrificer and his guests—and so on, until every part of the animal's anatomy is ritually assigned. If Dinka life were not this well ordered, Dinka society could not survive. The rules are not capricious; they are the end product of a long period of trial and error in learning to live in the swamps and river lands of the southern Nile.

But ecology—the relation of living things to the soil, the climate and the natural resources—is not the only key to the diversity of African societies. The innumerable ways in which men live together cannot be explained by environment alone. The Nyakyusa, a people who live in the flinty hills of Tanzania, obviously have a very different sort of land to contend with than the Dinka, and yet they are like the Dinka in some ways and unlike them in others. Just as the Dinka's life revolves around the campfire of the *wut*, so the Nyakyusa sets great store by fireside fellowship. In fact, they have a special name for it, *ukwangala*, "the enjoyment of good company." Monica Wilson, a South African anthropologist who has lived among them, says that *ukwangala* implies "urbane manners and a friendliness which expresses itself in eating and drinking together," and serves the purpose not only of "merry conversation, but also [of] discussion between equals, which the Nyakyusa regard as the principal form of education."

But the composition of Nyakyusa society is very different from that of the Dinka. While Dinka society is regulated by kinship, the Nyakyusa's system rests on age. The basic social unit is a village in which all the men are contemporaries. They may also, by chance, be brothers and cousins, but this relationship is incidental. The Nyakyusa's concern with age permeates his whole life. The boys who guard Nyakyusa fields and cattle live in separate camps or villages which become their social homes, although economically they are still members of their fathers' communities—caring for the family's cattle, working the family fields, and eating around the family campfire. When the members of a boy-village become old enough to marry, the village takes on a new character. Its houses become larger and farther apart, and the young men begin to cultivate more of the adjacent land. New boys applying for membership in the village are told to go away and start a boy-village of their own.

Other African societies living under similar circumstances do not find it necessary to divide themselves in this way. Why do the Nyakyusa? The answer apparently lies in the Nyakyusa beliefs about moral right and wrong, especially in the field of sex. They worry terribly about the problem of incest. Boys should not covet their mothers and aunts; fathers should leave their nieces and their sons' wives alone. "The seduction of young wives of an aging father is a common theme for scandal," writes Monica Wilson, "and a father's jealous fears are matched by those of his son."

At the same time, the Nyakyusa think it entirely proper for a man to have as many wives as he wants, as long as he can decently support them, and to marry them when they are quite young. Consequently Nyakyusa communities are perennially oversupplied with young bachelors, and short of attractive unmarried girls. The Nyakyusa's solution to this tense situation was worked out long ago: they decided to put fathers in one village and sons in another. Just as the Dinka arrived at a method for achieving social order out of economic necessity, so the Nyakyusa found a way to live in harmony despite a strict morality.

But how well did these self-regulating societies keep order outside their own immediate group? Did unrelated communities use the same method for resolving their differences? Apparently they did. Although warfare was not uncommon, it was nearly always warfare on a very small scale, conducted strictly according to convention. The notion that Africa was continually engulfed in great tribal wars is false.

No people, for instance, were more notorious for their military aggressiveness than the Zande, who lived in the high grasslands that divide the water-

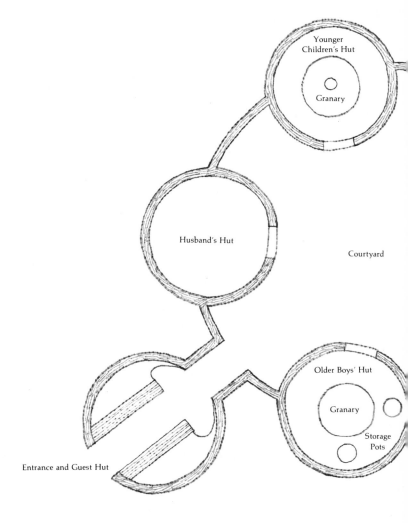

Younger Children's Hut

Granary

Husband's Hut

Courtyard

Older Boys' Hut

Granary

Storage Pots

Entrance and Guest Hut

shed of the Nile from the rivers of the northern Congo. They were said to fight with fanatical savagery, armed with multiblade throwing knives, and were suspected of eating their slain enemies. But only one European ever claimed to have witnessed such a Zande battle—an Italian traveler, Carlo Piaggia, who journeyed through the Zande lands in the middle of the 19th Century—and other visitors since then have found little to support this ugly reputation. British anthropologist E. E. Evans-Pritchard, who spent many years observing the Zande, describes their warfare as a carefully arranged confrontation that is designed to minimize the loss of life on both sides.

"I was told," writes Evans-Pritchard, "that since the aim was to get the enemy to withdraw so that

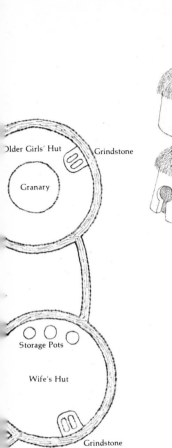

Older Girls' Hut   Grindstone

Granary

Storage Pots

Wife's Hut

Grindstone

A CIRCLE OF HUTS *is linked into a walled compound for protection from wild animals in the Sudan. Neatly built of mud with thatched roofs, the huts are sometimes crowned with gourds or ostrich eggs. The inward-facing units have raised, circular doorways to keep out rodents and domestic animals, but the main entrance is keyhole-shaped to allow easy access for people and provisions. Guests often sleep on ledges in this entrance building.*

Millet, the Nuba people's principal crop, is stored in circular granaries—earthenware jars so large that children are sometimes lowered inside them to ladle out grain. Beans, beer and other provisions are kept in small pots. The courtyard, often used to corral domestic animals, is also a center of communal activity. Here the Nuba family gathers to do chores, eat, and discuss the events of the day.

victory might be claimed with as little loss on your side as possible, you usually avoided complete encirclement, for if the enemy was unable to withdraw they would, seeing that there was no hope, sell their lives as dearly as they could. You therefore left a gap in the rear." Other rules of this kind included one that "fighting should begin about 4 o'clock in the afternoon, so that those who were getting the worst of it could withdraw under cover of darkness." In other words, the purpose of Zande warfare was not slaughter for the sake of slaughter. Wars were instruments of policy, undertaken to punish one's neighbor for a real or imagined wrong, or to rob him of his grain or marriageable girls. And a good deal of care was exercised to keep wars no bloodier than they had to be.

Among other African peoples wars were something to avoid and among one people—the Tallensi of northern Ghana—they were even considered sinful. Only when a very grave injury had been done one group by a member of another group did the Tallensi think fighting justified. These wars of reprisal seldom lasted more than a few days, and there were strong taboos against seizing the opponent's land or taking captives and booty. In addition, any food or livestock commandeered during the hostilities had to be eaten immediately or destroyed. All of this behavior was dictated by the intricacies of a social system which recognized ties not only of blood, but of place and sometimes of occupation. Every Tallensi group was usually related in some fashion or other to its neighbors, so that an act of aggression might involve a "brother." This was the main reason why war was a sin.

The Tallensi's elaborate kinship structure also regulated his society under less dramatic circumstances. In fact, the Tallensi are an excellent example of how a "simple society" with no apparent head, or central authority, keeps law and order. It did so through a whole series of interlocking checks and balances on the use of power, few of which were visible to outsiders. Early British administrators, discovering no sign of organized rule, assumed the Tallensi had none. "There was no one," says anthropologist Meyer Fortes, "who had authority over all the Tallensi; no one who could exact tax, tribute or service from all."

What the Tallensi did have, it was later perceived, was a network of social obligations that balanced one kind of power against another. Authority was vested in a number of men—the chiefs and priests responsible for various aspects of the Tallensi's religious, economic and political life. But the respective powers of these men were so great that they acted as restraints, making the men mutually dependent. This interdependence permeated Tallensi society, affecting the behavior of individuals, of groups and of communities of groups. The Tallensi being human, the system did not always function perfectly. Nevertheless, it produced a kind of self-propelled stability that made it possible for the Tallensi, a simple farming people who lived from their day-to-day labors, to avoid the major conflicts that could have spelled economic ruin.

For many African societies, however, the dangers of internally caused instability were nothing compared to the social disruption that followed in the wake of the slave trade. The chaos that so many Europeans claimed to find in Africa in the 19th Century was not illusion but dreadful reality. People were divided among themselves, driven from lands, pressured by a chain reaction of violence into patterns of life they had never known before. Even so, they survived—and often managed to build vigorous new societies upon the remnants of the old. In the little hills that lift in broken ranges from the shores of Lake Malawi in southeast Africa live a sturdy and ingenious people, the Lake Tonga, of whom this is especially true.

The Lake Tonga apparently came to their green and pleasant "land of the lake" a little over 150 years ago. Unlike their nearby neighbors, the Nyakyusa, who have lived for centuries with almost no contact with the rest of the world, the Lake Tonga were very much a product of external pressures. Probably they came from the northeast, from the country of inland Tanzania. One anthropologist who has studied them, Jaap van Velsen, believes they are a compound of several migrant groups who have managed to form themselves into a little "nation" of their own. This would help to explain their outgoing and enterprising character. The Lake Tonga are known far and wide across modern South Africa, and may be found in all sorts of occupations. They have produced, according to Van Velsen, "more than their fair share of trade union leaders, politicians and 'white collar' workers, including many in senior positions in the African civil service."

No doubt one reason for this is the Lake Tonga's early exposure to European education: there were teaching missionaries living among them in 1881, only a few decades after Dr. Livingstone's famous journey. But just as possibly, the Lake Tonga's venturesome nature resulted from social conditioning: the Tonga attach enormous importance to freedom of expression. Given two sets of kinship loyalties —to the villages and kinsmen of both his father and his mother—a Lake Tonga was free to move back and forth between them, changing allegiances as it suited him to do so, living wherever the economic situation was most attractive. He was also entirely free to express his personal quirks of temperament. Quarrels, arguments and disputes were, in fact, a regular feature of village life, and served, Van Velsen says, to strengthen rather than weaken the Tonga's sense of common identity. In them "the Tonga reaffirm and reanalyze the relationships" with their social unit. From long practice in coming to terms with each other, the Tonga have proved to be unusually skillful in manipulating people and situations in the outside world.

In the simple social order of village Africa, multiplied many times over, may be seen the fundamental truth about African life. Under its rough exterior, there is a sophisticated social sense that explains a great deal about the continent's history. Wildly raveled though it is, rich in memorable successes and by no means poor in crushing failures, offering the spectacle now of powerful empires, now of their sorry collapse, it is a history that never ceases to reveal two essential qualities: political skill and kinship loyalty. Upon these two qualities rested the conduct of civil affairs in simple villages like those of the Dinka and Tallensi, and complex empires like the one ruled from Zimbabwe.

NOVICE FIGHTERS, *resting in the crook of an old tree against an evening sky, watch a group of more experienced wrestlers practicing in a nearby field.*

THE WRESTLERS

Like many African peoples, the Nuba, who live in a remote, mountainous region of the Republic of the Sudan, have no written history. Their past, however, is strikingly preserved in traditions they have maintained for generations and probably centuries. Among two Nuba tribes in particular, the Korongo and the Mesakin, life in the villages centers on ceremonial wrestling, a ritual that goes back farther than tribal memory extends and is undoubtedly a dramatization of a more warlike past. Every boy who is physically fit spends his youth mastering the rules and movements of this art, preparing himself step by step for the championship matches that mark the culmination of a wrestler's career.

Wrestling among the Nuba is no more hostile than a contest between college teams; each man strives to win, but only for glory and symbolic prizes of twigs, the Nuba equivalent of Greek laurel wreaths. Yet to the cheering spectators, the great village matches embody all the skill, pride and continuity of the tribes.

THE BOYHOOD
HOME

Before a boy starts his arduous training as a wrestler, he lives with his family in the tribe's main village, in a compound much like the one at right—a collection of circular mud huts with thatched roofs built around a central court. When his father thinks he is ready to try his skill at wrestling, usually about the age of 13 or 14, the boy is sent to an all-male camp several miles from the village. Here, in high hopes of earning glory and his eventual place in the tribe, he devotes almost all of his energies and thoughts to learning the art of wrestling from older boys and men.

Until he reaches marriageable age, the young wrestler spends half of every year at the wrestling camp and only visits home to fight in exhibition matches, to pick up supplies or to help with the harvest. When he does marry, he must leave the camp and give up wrestling: a wife, the Nuba firmly believe, saps a man of the strength to fight. He returns to the village, builds his homestead, and turns to the business of farming and bringing up his own sons.

ON THE PRACTICE FIELD *two children of the lowest wrestling rank circle each other as they try to find a hold. Their beads, shaved heads and feathers are all traditional parts of a wrestler's costume which each boy may vary according to his taste; only at matches must he wear prescribed decorations.*

STEPS ON THE ROAD TO MANHOOD

Although most candidates begin their training as wrestlers when they are about 13, a boy of exceptional strength and character may start when he is younger. He immediately enters the first of four ranks through which he must pass before he can become a full-fledged fighter. Besides wrestling, he must tend the village's herd of cattle.

In early adolescence, after he has learned the basic wrestling holds, his father, by custom, promotes him to the second rank by announcing, "The boy has grown strong; it is time to dress him." In a simple ceremony the father ties four strips of white cloth around the neck and waist of his son,

who is then permitted to take part in informal matches with members of his new rank.

The ritual that marks entrance into the third rank is more elaborate. Many neighbors and relatives come to the home of the boy's family in the village; a male goat is cooked and quantities of beer are served. After the father invests his son with the regalia of the third rank *(above, right)*, the boy, usually about 16 years old at this point, is ready for his first serious public match. Just before he leaves his family's hut for the ring, some of the older male guests put on a jovial practice fight to reveal to him the fine points of the art.

DURING INITIATION RITES *a young wrestler, who has covered his hair with wet ashes, stands with his arms raised as bolts of cloth are wrapped around his waist. Later he will receive cow and goat tails which he will attach to his wide ceremonial wrestling belt.*

PREPARING FOR BATTLE, *a wrestler of the highest rank paints his body and shaved head with ashes mixed in milk. The ashes provide the wrestler with a better grip, and the cattle-raising Nuba believe that the milk gives the wrestler strength in competition.*

THE STRUGGLE FOR GLORY

After years of preparation a wrestler joins the fourth and highest rank. Only then may he enter the tournaments that are held among the best fighters from many neighboring villages. Before these matches messengers run through the hills

blowing horns to summon an audience. Friends give the opponents last-minute blessings and help them fasten on their heavy cowtail belts. The contenders, covered with ceremonial ashes, enter the ring and circle each other in stylized steps. Suddenly one of the wrestlers attacks and tries to throw the other man down. When he finally pins both his opponent's shoulders to the ground, the victor is hoisted aloft by his cheering friends and carried through the village in triumph.

DEATH OF A HERO

The respect the Nuba have for their champion wrestlers is never more clearly demonstrated than when one of them dies in his prime. Grief sweeps the community. Thousands of tribesmen pour into the village to pay their last respects, some carrying ceremonial leather fans with which they beat up dust from the ground as they make their way to the funeral hut. While mourners file past the athlete, his fellow wrestlers intone a prayer; first one man chants a verse and then the chorus repeats it. Outside the hut dancers move in stunned silence. All through the night sentries stand a solemn watch, their bodies painted with skeleton designs.

A MOURNING MOTHER *sits beside her dead son. After friends and relatives bid farewell to the deceased they sprinkle ashes on his hand, which is the only exposed part of his body, and leave behind gifts such as the chicken by his side.*

COMMUNING WITH A SPIRIT, *a Nuba girl closes her eyes, which she has painted white so she can see the departed man. The lip ring she wears is an ancient decoration now found only in remote areas.*

WEARY SENTINELS *keep vigil near the funeral hut all day and night. Many of them had been the dead man's close friends since they progressed through the ranks together in wrestling school.*

THE SACRIFICE
BY THE GRAVE

On the day of the wrestler's funeral a herd of cattle is brought from the wrestling camp to the village, where it will be ceremonially slaughtered as an offering at his grave. A fellow athlete, chosen for his physical prowess and virtue, dons pink feathers as the sign of his sacred office and begins to kill the cattle. He thrusts a spear into the heart of each animal and cuts off the tail, ears and horns, which are distributed among the dead man's friends; the foreleg is boiled and put into the grave. Sometimes as many as 50 cattle are sacrificed and eaten during the funeral feast; to afford so many animals some poor families incur debts that last for generations.

After the slaughter the tribesmen stage a major wrestling tournament in honor of the deceased; often a new wrestling ground is established near the grave, where similar memorial contests are held every year. Finally, the hero is buried, and cattle horns filled with ashes are placed above him to give him strength as he makes his journey toward the Nuba's land of the dead.

سَرُوجُ يَا أَنِقْ فَسِيرِي وَخُذِي
وَادَّجِي وَأَوِّي إِلَى أُسَيِّدِي

حَتَّى نَطَأَ خَفَّالِمُرَعَاهَا النَّدِي
فَتَرْعَى جَبِيدٌ وَتَسْعَدِي

وَمَا مُنَى أَنْ تَنْهَمِي وَتَنْجُدِي
أَبِهِ فَبَيْنَكَ النَّوْقُ وَجْدِي وَاجْهَدِي

وَأَرْىَ أَدِيمٌ فَدْفَدٍ فَفَدْفَدٍ
وَاقْنَعِي بِالنَّتْجِ عِنْدَا الْمَوْرِدِ

وَلَا تَحِطِّي دُونَ ذَالِ الْمَقْصَدِ
فَقَدْ جَلَفْتِ جِلْفَهُ لِلْمُجْنَدِي

4
MERCHANT EMPIRES

The songs and folk tales of Africa contain many brilliant memories of a golden past—of an age of kingdoms and heroes, of men who were warriors, statesmen, magicians. These songs and stories still have the power to bring old men together and enchant the young, for they carry their listeners back to another Africa, overleaping the sad humiliations of colonial rule. Great occasions especially call them forth, but even in a casual gathering a singer can command a responsive audience.

One evening in recent times at a remote upcountry inn in the new Republic of Guinea, a group of travelers witnessed such a performance. As they sat conversing in the common room of the inn there appeared at the door a young woman, handsome and self-assured, with a flash of filigree in ears and hair. She seated herself among the company, spread wide her skirts, settled her infant daughter and began to sing of Guinea's history.

She sang first of the architect of the young republic's freedom, Sékou Touré, of his energy and courage in the struggle for independence. But her song soon took her back across the years to another Touré, the dour and stubborn 19th Century leader Samori ibn Lafiya, who resisted the French invasion of West Africa for more than 16 years and is remembered with a mixture of admiration and despair. From Samori she went far deeper into the past, to sing of Askia Muhammad Touré, Askia the Great, who ruled the wide West African empire of Songhai in the 16th Century and made the rich city of Timbuktu a center of learning.

Today Timbuktu is a modest provincial town in the Republic of Mali, far off the beaten track and much reduced in honor and wealth. Nothing there suggests literary distinction, or indeed any kind of eminence. Yet in Askia Muhammad's time the Muslim scholar Leo Africanus visited Timbuktu with a diplomatic mission and reported that it "has a splendid and well-organized royal court, many craftsmens' shops, and markets where European cloth is sold."

Other visitors confirmed Leo's impression. One of them was Mahmud al-Kati, who in 1519 began to collect the notes for a history which he called the *Tarikh al-Fettash*, the "chronicle of the researcher." Al-Kati was then about 51 years old.

ARAB TRADERS, *like the one in this 13th Century drawing, journeyed south across the Sahara to the great kingdoms of the Western Sudan. Astride their camels, they could cross 200 miles of desert in a week.*

As a young man he had the good fortune to win Askia Muhammad's patronage, and accompanied him on a pilgrimage to Mecca. When they returned to Timbuktu, al-Kati served the King in various official capacities, earning the honorable title of *alfa* (doctor of law). He lived to a great age —possibly, the evidence suggests, 125. Thus he witnessed the whole of the 16th Century, when the Songhai empire was at the peak of its fame. But more than that, al-Kati was a Soninke, a descendant of the people who had ruled the ancient empire of Ghana many centuries before—and so he was in a position to know the old traditions as well as contemporary history.

The King who ruled ancient Ghana, said al-Kati, possessed 1,000 horses, each of which had its own mattress, its own copper urinal and three servants. This king's name was Kanissa'ai and he was "one of the lords of the gold." Every evening the King came out of his palace to talk with his subjects, but only after "a thousand faggots were gathered for a fire, so that all might be lit and warmed." The flames of this fire lit up "the space between heaven and earth." Then he would seat himself "upon a balcony of red-gleaming gold" and order his servants "to bring forth food sufficient for 10,000 people."

Much of this is legend, no doubt; yet how much is truth? In the 11th Century—just a few years after William of Normandy conquered England at the Battle of Hastings in 1066—a great Spanish-Arab geographer, al-Bakri of Córdoba, compiled his *Book of Roads and Kingdoms*, a sort of African gazetteer. In it al-Bakri set down an account of the court ceremony of a King of Ghana that is not too different from the one described by al-Kati. When the King "gives an audience to his people, in order to listen to their complaints and set them right," wrote al-Bakri, "he sits in a pavilion around which stand 10 horses with gold-embroidered trappings. Behind the king stand 10 pages holding shields and gold-mounted swords; on his right are the sons of princes of his empire, splendidly clad and with gold plaited in their hair. . . . The door of the pavilion is guarded by dogs of an excellent breed who almost never leave the king's presence, and who wear collars of gold and silver."

The authenticity of al-Bakri's account is confirmed in part by the statistics in his book, giving the distances between cities and markets. Many of these can be checked, and they are very accurate. He is also supported by the discoveries of archeologists. Al-Bakri described Ghana's capital, for example, as a city composed of two towns lying on a plain. One was inhabited by Muslim merchants, the other by the king and his court. The Muslim town possessed 12 mosques, staffed by salaried Koranic readers and men of learning, and around it were "wells of sweet water from which they drink and near which they grow vegetables." The king's compound, six miles distant, had "a palace and a number of dome-shaped dwellings, the whole surrounded by an enclosure like the defensive wall of a city."

The ruins of what was almost certainly the first of these towns were identified by a French colonial administrator, Albert Bonnel de Mézières, in 1914. They are at a place known as Kumbi Salih, in Mauritania, some 200 miles north of the modern city of Bamako, in the Republic of Mali. Excavating these ruins in the early 1950s, French archeologists Raymond Mauny and Paul Thomassey laid bare a number of fine stone houses, some of them two stories high—clearly the dwellings of al-Bakri's prosperous Muslim merchants.

The legends of the Western Sudan, then, are based on truth; they embroider but they do not invent. They are highlights in the histories of a series of great commercial empires that flourished in the wide grasslands of north-central Africa from the

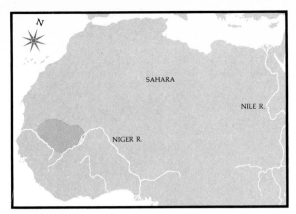

GHANA *(700-1200 A.D.) was the first great Sudanese empire.*

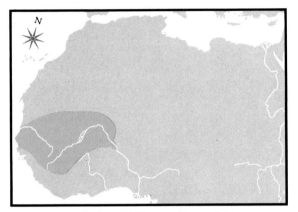

MALI *(1200-1500) absorbed Ghana and extended it westward.*

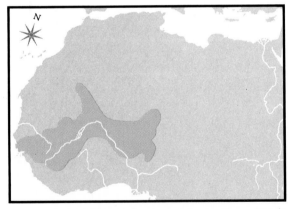

SONGHAI *(1350-1600) slowly usurped the territory of Mali.*

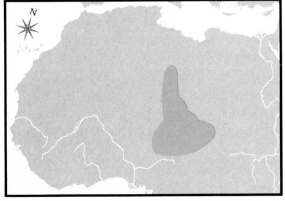

KANEM-BORNU *(800-1800) grew separately in the interior.*

FOUR TRADING EMPIRES, *shown in the maps at left, flourished in the Sudan starting about the Eighth Century. They grew prosperous mainly by importing salt mined in the north, which they traded for gold from local mines.*

Eighth Century until just before colonial times.

The first of these empires was the kingdom of Ghana, which apparently rose in the western region of the Sudan some time around 700 and disappeared in the 13th Century. The second was the empire of Mali, which followed upon Ghana in much the same region but evolved into a far larger political system over a wider area. Emerging in the 13th Century, Mali declined in the 15th Century and came to an end 100 years later. Overlapping Mali in time was a third empire, the kingdom of Songhai, which dated from roughly 1350 to 1600, and extended farther eastward, toward Lake Chad.

If modern folk singers of the Western Sudan look back upon these empires as a golden age, they do so with good reason. Much of the empires' wealth and power was derived quite literally from gold. This was the strength of Ghana, and afterward of Mali. It was the reason for the rise of Songhai, and also the cause of its fall—attracting a catastrophic Moroccan invasion in 1591 which left the empire in ruins. The trans-Saharan gold trade went far back in time, to the days of Phoenician settlements along the North African coast, but its heyday began with the Muslim Arab conquest of North Africa in the Seventh and Eighth Centuries and an influx of Muslim merchants.

From the time of Ghana onward, the West African merchant cities exploited their advantageous middleman positions in this renewed commerce, dominating the export of gold to the north and the import of salt, the "prince of commodities," to the hot and desalinated regions of inner Africa. "In the sands of that country is gold, treasure inexpressible," wrote one Spanish traveler, Abu Hamid al-Andalusi. "Merchants trade with salt for it, taking the salt on camels from the salt mines. They start from a town called Sijilmasa . . . and travel in the desert as it were upon the sea, having guides to pilot them by the stars or rocks.

. . . They take provisions for six months, and when they reach Ghana they weigh their salt and sell it against a certain unit of weight of gold . . . according to the market and the supply."

As time went by, these cities amassed great wealth. Writing in the 10th Century, the Arab geographer Ibn Hawqal remarked that a merchant in Sijilmasa owed his partner in the Saharan city of Awdoghast the immense sum of 40,000 golden dinars (a dinar was the weight of 72 grains of barley). At about the same time the peoples of these regions came under the influence of Mohammedanism. With the new religion arrived the techniques of literacy, the traditions of learning, a code of laws, and the usages of currency and credit. Gradually the cities' inhabitants acquired urban habits of comfort, leisure and education. Al-Bakri, in his *Book of Roads and Kingdoms*, described Awdoghast as "a very large city with several markets, many date palms and henna trees as large as olive trees . . . filled with fine houses and solid buildings." He also spoke enthusiastically about the charms of its women.

Not all the accounts of the African kingdoms were this glowing. One of the most famous and extensive of them was composed by Ibn Battuta, a Berber scholar and theologian from Tangier. Ibn Battuta crossed the Sahara in 1352 and spent about a year in the kingdom of Mali, which by this time had supplanted Ghana as the dominant force in the Sudan. On his way south Ibn Battuta paused for a while in the "salt city" of Taghaza, which he described as "an unattractive village, with the curious feature that its houses and mosques are built of blocks of salt, roofed with camel skins. There are no trees there, nothing but sand. In the sand is a salt mine; they dig for the salt and find it in thick slabs, lying one on top of the other, as though they had been tool-squared and laid under the surface of the earth."

South of the Sahara, Ibn Battuta stayed for a time in the market city of Walata, on the northern border of the Mali empire. He found the people strange, and their manners often deplorable. He was deeply upset, or so he claimed, by the freedom of the physical relations that existed between the sexes. "The women there," he wrote, "have 'friends' and 'companions' amongst the men outside their own families, and the men in the same way have 'companions' amongst the women of other families. One day at Walata I went into the judge's house, after asking his permission, and found with him a young woman of remarkable beauty. I was shocked and turned to go out, but . . . the judge said to me: 'Why are you going out? She is my companion.' I was amazed . . . for he was a theologian and a pilgrim to boot."

Ibn Battuta was also offended by the apparent meanness of African hospitality. At Walata he was invited to dinner by a city official who served him pounded millet mixed with milk and honey in a half calabash. "Was it for this that the black invited us?" he asked, and the reply was, "Yes; it is in their opinion the highest form of hospitality." Later, in the capital of Mali, he complained that the Sultan was "a miserly king, not a man from whom one may hope for a rich present." Instead of the "robes of honor and money" that Ibn Battuta expected, he got "three cakes of bread, a piece of beef fried in native oil, and a calabash of sour curds."

On questions of more substance, however, Ibn Battuta rendered a more favorable judgment. Among the admirable qualities of the people, he noted a high sense of justice. "Of all peoples, the Negroes are those who most abhor injustice. The Sultan pardons no one who is guilty of it. There is complete and general safety throughout the land. The traveler here has no more reason than the man who stays at home to fear brigands, thieves or ravishers." Furthermore, said Ibn Battuta, "the blacks do

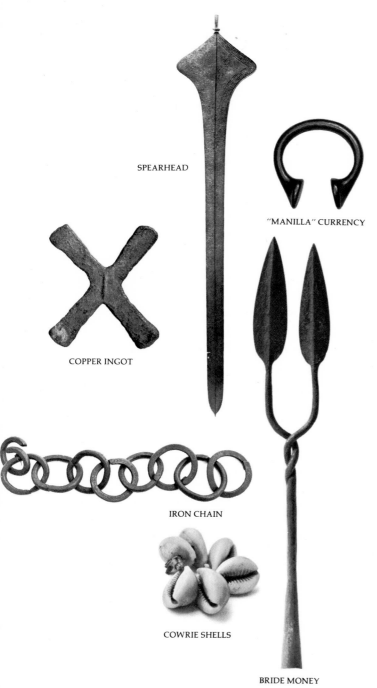

SPEARHEAD

"MANILLA" CURRENCY

COPPER INGOT

IRON CHAIN

COWRIE SHELLS

BRIDE MONEY

AFRICAN CURRENCY *once ranged from cattle to gold, from salt to slaves, but as trading empires grew, standardized money appeared. With beads or spearheads the African could buy food and clothing; for an agreed-upon number of shells, goats or special "bride-price objects" he could purchase a wife.*

not confiscate the goods of any North Africans who may die in their country, not even when these consist of large treasures. On the contrary, they deposit these goods with a man of confidence . . . until those who have a right to the goods present themselves and take possession."

Like al-Bakri, who had been impressed by the court ceremonial of 11th Century Ghana, Ibn Battuta was impressed by the pomp and circumstance of royal audiences in 14th Century Mali. However inappropriate the Sultan's gifts might seem, his authority was not to be denied. On official audience days, said Ibn Battuta, the Sultan emerged from his palace "preceded by his musicians, who carry gold and silver *guimbris* [two-stringed guitars], and behind him come 300 armed slaves." Dressed in a "velvety red tunic" and a golden skullcap, he ascended to a platform carpeted with silk and sheltered from the blazing sun by a large umbrella, "which is a sort of pavilion made of silk, surmounted by a bird fashioned in gold about the size of a falcon." His progress to this platform was leisurely, and he mounted it "in the sedate manner of a preacher ascending the pulpit of a mosque," while drums beat and bugles sounded.

No other account of the empire of Mali has anything like the savory detail of Ibn Battuta's memoir, but he was not the only man to write about it. In fact, the news of the wealth and splendor of Mali had spread far and wide, mainly as a result of the pilgrimage to Mecca in 1324 of Mansa Musa, the greatest of all the Mali emperors. Musa was accompanied, it was said, by a retinue of 60,000 men, including 500 slaves, each of whom bore a bar of gold weighing 500 *mitqals*, the equivalent of about four pounds.

Even allowing for exaggeration, it is clear that Musa's pilgrimage caused a sensation. In Cairo the value of the local dinar was depressed for at least 12 years by Musa's openhandedness with his

Sudanese gold. But his Egyptian hosts also remembered him for his pride. "I suggested," one recalled, "that he should go up to the palace and meet the Sultan. But he refused. He said, 'I came for the pilgrimage and nothing else.' I well understood that the meeting was repugnant to him because he was loath to kiss the ground [before the Sultan] or kiss his hand." Musa finally agreed to this formality, but declared that, on kissing the ground, "I will prostrate myself before Allah who created me and brought me into the world."

His stubbornness can be understood. Mali, after all, was far bigger than Egypt, and its wealth was far greater—at least when measured in gold. Musa's domains stretched from the waters of the Atlantic along the northern coast of modern Senegal to the boundaries of modern Nigeria, and from the fringe of the rain forests on the south to the oasis markets of the central Sahara. After the Mongol Empire in Asia, it was the biggest imperial system of its day. Sheik Uthman ed-Dukkali, a learned Egyptian who lived in Mali for 35 years, declared that it was "four months of travel long and four months wide."

As late as 1500, when Mali's power had already been superseded by Songhai's, another famous traveler provided a more detailed description of Mali. Leo Africanus, the Spanish Muslim whose real name was Hassan Ibn Muhammad, described the capital of Mali as a town of 6,000 dwellings and several mosques and Islamic schools. Its people, Leo said, were artisans and merchants dealing in a wide range of products, and superior to "all other Negroes in wit, civility and industry."

It was Leo also who described Timbuktu when that city was the cultural capital of the Songhai empire. By Leo's time cities such as Timbuktu and Jenne had acquired a reputation for learning and scholarly hospitality throughout the Muslim world. Erudite Muslims traveled to them to add another dimension to their minds: African scholars might take their doctrines from Cairo but their ideas were their own. They gathered around them students and disciples, and wrote prolifically in all the customary forms of Islamic literature—biographies and histories, religious commentaries and legal dissertations, the correspondence of judges and kings. Some of their work acquired an almost classical authority and is still used today in Koranic schools in the Western Sudan. The libraries of these scholars were the reason for Leo's remark that in Timbuktu the book trade provided a better source of profit than any other kind of commerce.

Leo's stories excited the whole of trading Europe, but the stories were not generally circulated until a half century later. Some time after he returned from the Sudan, Leo was captured by Christian pirates on the Mediterranean and taken to Rome as an odd and distinguished prisoner. He was received by Pope Leo X, who was so delighted with the Moor's learning that he christened him with his own name—and gave him a pension that allowed Leo to set down the account of his African travels.

Long before this book appeared, however, distant echoes of the African empires' wealth and trading enterprise had begun to find their way to the medieval merchant cities of southern Europe. Several of them, notably Marseilles, Genoa, Florence, Venice, had long made efforts to penetrate the Muslim barrier of North Africa and link their commerce with the Western Sudan. Sometimes they even tried to reach the empires by sea. In 1346 a Catalan captain named Jacme Ferrer set out in a galley from Majorca to find "the river of gold" which was thought to lie somewhere far down the Atlantic coast. But Ferrer never came back. Europeans possessed as yet neither the necessary skill nor instruments for ocean voyaging.

In 1375 another Majorcan, the cartographer Abraham Cresques, produced a map of the "unknown continent" from information probably given to him by his fellow Jews, who, unlike Christian merchants, were often permitted by the Muslims in North Africa to journey through their territory. Among other things, Cresques' map showed the mighty "Lord of the Negroes" seated on his throne in the midst of Mali, bearing aloft a ceremonial orb of gold. A white-veiled merchant rode toward him down the long Saharan camel trails.

Another event several decades later suggests that quite a few bold souls did in fact follow where Cresques pointed. In 1413 a man called Anselm d'Isalguier came safely home to Marseilles and Toulouse, bringing with him an African princess for a wife and a train of African servants—one of whom set himself up as a doctor and enormously irritated the French medical profession by treating no less a person than the Dauphin Charles, heir to the throne of France.

The most persistent efforts to penetrate Africa by land, however, were made by the Italian city-states. Not long after d'Isalguier's return, the Genoese managed to establish a man called Antonio Malfante in the Saharan oasis town of Tuat. A little later the great Florentine banking house of Portinari was even more successful—its agent, Benedetto Dei, actually got through to Timbuktu and set up business contacts. Not surprisingly, in those days of highly competitive enterprise, the bankers and merchants kept their information to themselves—so well, in fact, that most of their African agents' reports are entirely lost to posterity.

Meanwhile, with the benefit of better sails and instruments, the Portuguese began pushing down the long Atlantic coast sometime after 1430, attempting to establish their own African contacts by sea. There were Portuguese ships in West African waters by the 1440s. But again, most of the information their crews obtained was considered a state secret and was hidden in the royal archives. Not until 1550 did any detailed account of the

THE RICHES OF GAO: AN EXPLORER'S ACCOUNT

In a time when Columbus was sailing to the New World, the Moorish explorer and scholar Leo Africanus was visiting the kingdoms of western Africa. His major work, "The History and Description of Africa," contains this report of the opulent capital of Songhai:

"Gao is a very large city similar to Kabara, that is, without surrounding walls. The city is about 650 kilometers from Timbuktu to the southeast. Most of its houses are ugly; however, a few, in which live the king and his court, have a very fine aspect. Its inhabitants are rich merchants who travel constantly about the region with their wares. A great many Blacks come to the city bringing quantities of gold with which to purchase goods imported from the Berber country and from Europe, but they never find enough goods on which to spend all their gold and always take half or two-thirds of it home.

"The city is well-policed in comparison to Timbuktu. Bread and meat exist in great abundance, but one can find neither wine nor fruit. In truth, melons, cucumbers, and excellent pumpkins are abundant and they have enormous quantities of rice. Freshwater wells are numerous. There is a place where they sell countless . . . slaves on market days. A fifteen-year-old girl is worth about six ducats and a young man nearly as much; little children and aged slaves are worth about half that sum.

"The king has a special palace set aside for women, concubines, and slaves, and for the eunuchs charged with watching over these women. He has . . . a necessary guard of horsemen and of foot-soldiers armed with bows. Between the public gate and the private door to his palace is a great courtyard surrounded by a wall. A gallery on each side of this courtyard is used for holding audiences. Even though the king handles all his affairs himself, he is aided by many functionaries, such as secretaries, advisors, captains, and stewards."

IVORY, GOLD AND SALT, *three of Africa's major products, were keystones of the great trading empires. Elephant tusks (below), exported from the east coast, were the source of almost all of the world's ivory. Gold coins (center) were used as currency in the north, and cylinders of salt (right) mined in the Sahara were traded extensively in the south.*

West African empires become generally available to the European public. In that year, mainly for the benefit of his native city, a former secretary in the Venetian government, Giovanni Battista Ramusio, published Leo Africanus' report to Pope Leo X.

For Ramusio, and soon for others, the message was clear: the merchants of Europe should "go and do business with the king of Timbuktu and Mali." In this realm they would find hospitality and useful markets. Leo spoke of cities like Gao, Timbuktu, Katsina and Kano, which were already dealing through North African intermediaries in the fabrics and metalware of Europe. Obviously these cities were centers of powerful states. In Guangara, for example, said Leo, the King had an army of 7,000 archers and 500 cavalry, drew great revenues from trade and taxation, and ruled over "many rich people." Furthermore, added Leo, Guangara was only one of many African states that valued the goods of Europe and offered such things as gold and ivory for easy purchase.

By the end of the 16th Century, European maritime interests were confirming Leo's account. Por-

tugal was buying gold at several points along the West African coast, and in 1555 an English expedition anchored in the Thames with a cargo of 400 pounds of gold and 250 ivory tusks, comfortably multiplying its capital investment many times over. Other Englishmen quickly followed, returning with equally satisfactory results. Subsequently, in 1561, Queen Elizabeth herself invested in African trade and cleared a profit on one voyage of £1,000.

It is not too much to say that the prosperity of the African trading empires between the 13th and 16th Centuries was in a large measure caused by Europe's demand for more gold. Partly through an increase in trade, partly through a cutting off of traditional sources of supply, the gold reserves of Europe were drying up.

Actually the traders who bargained for African gold never knew precisely where it came from. Those who pushed down from the north by caravan knew only that it came from somewhere south of Timbuktu and Gao. Those who anchored off the coast were told that it came from somewhere in the north. There were in fact two main gold regions. The older, linked to the rise of ancient Gha-

na and Mali, lay in the northern part of what is now the Republic of Guinea. Toward 1400, however, the expanding demand for gold prompted the rise of a second and eventually more important gold region, in the forest lands of modern Ghana.

Technologically, the mining and working of this gold was entirely an African development—none of the methods of prospecting were imported from outside. Some of the gold was alluvial and could be panned from the rivers without much difficulty. But much of it was embedded in seams and had to be mined. Hundreds of shafts were opened, varying from a few feet to almost 100 feet deep, the latter being linked by galleries and side shafts. Extraction was undoubtedly crude and laborious —the ore was hacked out and crushed by hand— but the results were impressive. The total amount mined from antiquity until 1500 is estimated to have been about 3,500 tons.

Not all of Africa's gold moved north through the desert or west to the Atlantic coast. Far over to the east, another great system of interlocking states, also based on trade, rose and flourished on the demand for gold—but not just for gold alone. Merchants from Arabia and India put in their ships along the coasts of what are now Somalia, Kenya and Tanzania to carry away gold, ivory, iron, tortoise shell and slaves. This east coast trade, too, had begun in very ancient times. In the Second or Third Century an anonymous author published a sailors' guide, written in Greek, which describes coastal conditions in the Red Sea and Indian Ocean as far south as modern Tanzania. "Much ivory is taken away from these places," says the author, "and also rhinoceros horn and tortoise shell."

Over the centuries this trade expanded, mostly through the enterprise of Muslim merchants—although there are indications that at least two large Chinese fleets may have brought their towering hulls to anchor off the shores of East Africa. This

A MOST EXOTIC PRODUCT, a giraffe from the African kingdom of Malindi arrived in China in 1415. This strange, long-necked creature so impressed the Chinese emperor he ordered a fleet to escort the ambassadors from Malindi safely home.

commerce brought into being comfortable cities, among the richest of which was Kilwa. "Kilwa is one of the most beautiful and well-constructed towns in the world. The whole of it is elegantly built," wrote Ibn Battuta—the same Battuta who later visited Mali. And in 1961 British archeologist Neville Chittick uncovered the evidence of Kilwa's onetime wealth and sophistication. Under the shroud of looming trees and sweltering undergrowth, he came upon the ghostly ruins of its royal palace, Husuni Kubwa, an enormous structure of well over 100 rooms, with galleries, patios, elaborate washing arrangements and a fresh-water bathing pool.

Like its sister trading cities, Kilwa's function was essentially that of middleman. Its merchant rulers (who called themselves sultans) controlled the exchange of goods between inner Africa and the Arabian and Indian trading ships that plied the coast. For themselves and their African partners, the merchants of Kilwa bought Eastern fabrics, beads, porcelain and other luxuries; in return, they sold gold, ivory, copper and iron. Their application to this trade was ferocious. Inland, Kilwa's trading contacts reached Lake Nyasa, and may even have extended to the empire of Mali—on the other side of the continent. Along the coast it dominated commerce to the south, as far as Sofala, 900 miles away.

Kilwa had a mint, the first in Africa, and at the height of its affluence its sultans cast coins in several denominations, possibly as many as six. In addition, it milked the Arab and Indian traders with stiff and unrelenting duties and tariffs. Part of this money was used to reinforce its power over neighboring territories, but Kilwa's wealth also went into the embellishment of its daily life. When the Portuguese first sailed into Kilwa's harbor in 1500 under the command of Pedro Alvares Cabral, they marveled at its fine houses of coral stone, many of them three and four stories high—"like those of Spain," reported the anonymous scribe who accompanied Cabral. They were also amazed by its people: "In this land there are rich merchants," wrote the same scribe, "and there is much gold and silver and amber and musk and pearls. Those of the land wear clothes of fine cotton and of silk and many fine things, and they are black men."

But for all their stiff trading habits, the merchants of Kilwa—and of the other east coast market cities, Mombasa, Malindi, Kisimani-Mafia, Mogadishu, and the like—performed a valuable service. Just as the trans-Saharan trade stitched together the West African hinterland into powerful empires, so the Indian Ocean coastal trade helped to link the peoples who lived on the wide plateau of central Africa—stretching from modern Zambia down through Rhodesia—into strong kingdoms and confederacies.

Of these interior African kingdoms the most successful were two that flourished in sequence in the region for which Zimbabwe became an important market town and religious center. The first of these empires rose to power in 1440, under the rule of a king named Mutota, whose honorary title, Monomotapa, gave the empire its name. The Portuguese knew Zimbabwe under its Monomotapa rulers as the chief collection point for the gold brought out to the coast. In 1518 a Portuguese agent, Duarte Barbosa, reported that the Monomotapa ruler was "a great lord, with many kings under him." Later this empire was ruled by another dynasty of lords, the Rozwi; it was they who raised the Great Temple of Zimbabwe, a royal enclosure with walls rising as high as 32 feet. Thus, by the 16th Century, no large region of Africa remained untouched by the economic and political pressures of external trade, and no large region had failed to produce evidence, often varied and contrasting, of internal growth.

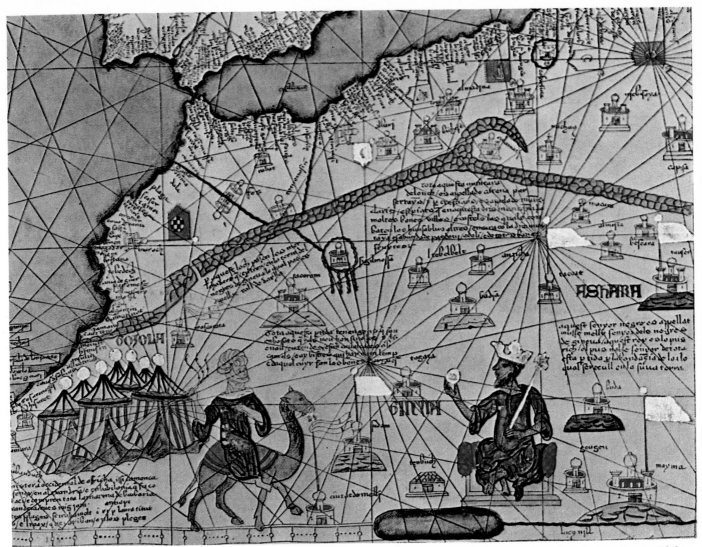

"THE RICHEST KING IN AFRICA," *Mansa Musa of Mali holds a huge gold nugget in this 1375 Catalan map as an Arab trader rides in to barter with him.*

A NETWORK OF COMMERCE

In the precolonial era, Africa's internal trade—as well as its commerce with Europe and the East—was as highly organized as any system known today. Ships from Spain, Portugal and Italy called regularly at Africa's Mediterranean ports, where European cargoes of cloth, horses and manufactured items were exchanged for dates, olives, kola nuts, cotton, copper and—above all—gold, the indispensable basis of the African economy. Africa's products reached the markets in a variety of ways: on the backs of donkeys and camels, on the heads of porters, in the holds of barges and sailing boats. Africans maintained not only their brisk inland trade, but also a prosperous overseas business with India and the Orient. In the marketplace, too, African traders proved their bargaining mettle, often sending their European counterparts home with new respect for their business acumen.

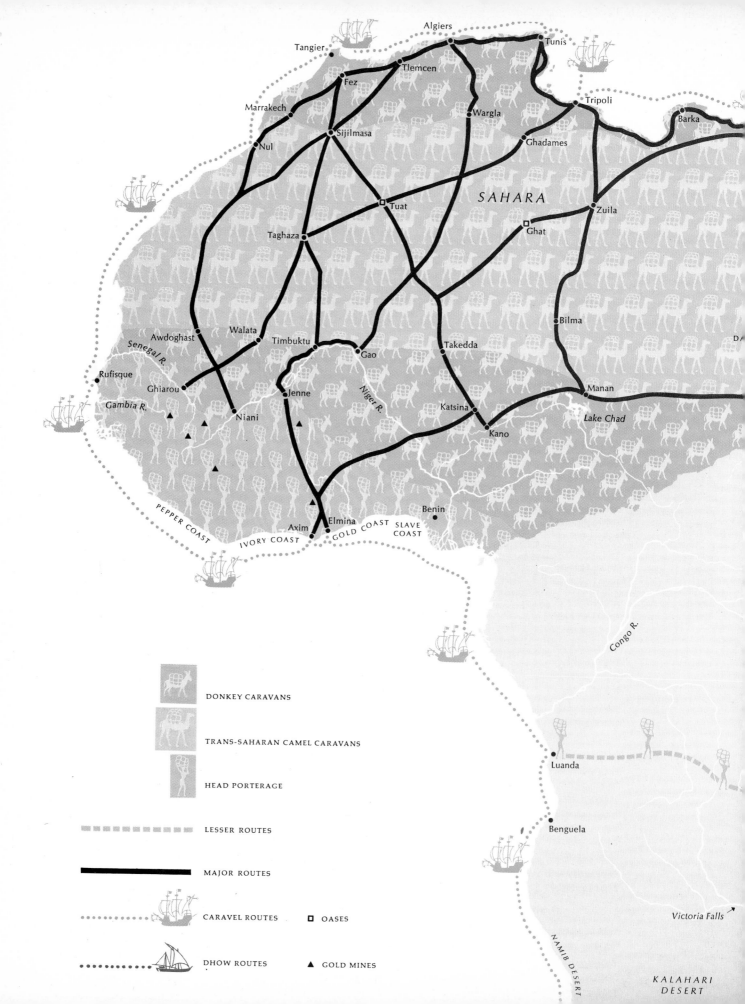

Tangier

Algiers
Tunis
Tripoli
Tlemcen
Fez
Barka
Marrakech
Sijilmasa
Nul
Wargla
Ghadames
SAHARA
Tuat
Zuila
Taghaza
Ghat
Bilma
Awdoghast
Walata
Timbuktu
Gao
Takedda
Senegal R.
Manan
Rufisque
Ghiarou
Jenne
Niger R.
Katsina
Lake Chad
Gambia R.
Niani
Kano

PEPPER COAST
Axim   Elmina
Benin
IVORY COAST   GOLD COAST   SLAVE COAST

Congo R.

DONKEY CARAVANS

TRANS-SAHARAN CAMEL CARAVANS

HEAD PORTERAGE

Luanda

LESSER ROUTES

MAJOR ROUTES

Benguela

CARAVEL ROUTES   ☐ OASES

Victoria Falls

DHOW ROUTES   ▲ GOLD MINES

NAMIB DESERT

KALAHARI
DESERT

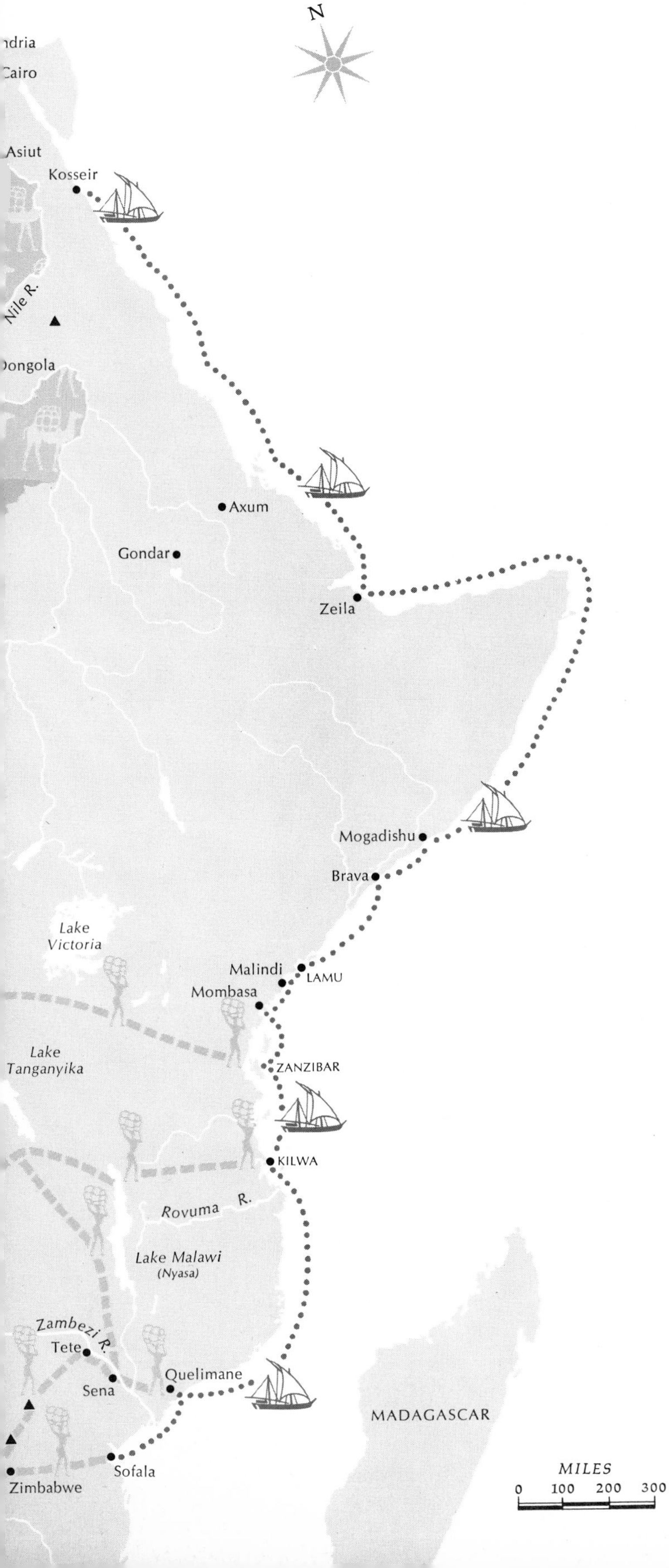
N
Kosseir
Asiut
Nile R.
Axum
Gondar
Zeila
Mogadishu
Brava
Lake Victoria
Malindi
LAMU
Mombasa
Lake Tanganyika
ZANZIBAR
KILWA
Rovuma R.
Lake Malawi (Nyasa)
Zambezi R.
Tete
Sena
Quelimane
Sofala
Zimbabwe
MADAGASCAR
MILES
0 100 200 300

FAR-FLUNG ROUTES OF TRADE

After European products arrived at Africa's north coast, they were carried by donkeys through the verdant coastal lands. The donkey trains converged at inland "ports"—principally Sijilmasa, Marrakech and Ghadames—along the northern border of the Sahara, and returned to the coast with products brought across the desert from the south.

The bulk of the products bound for central Africa was loaded onto camels, and then sent off along an intricate network of caravan routes across the desert wastes. On the southern rim of the Sahara another group of "ports"—Timbuktu, Walata, Gao, Takedda—awaited the caravans, and another exchange took place. While the camels, now laden with hides, kola nuts and gold, set out on the return journey, the European products they had brought across the desert continued south through the forests, borne on the heads of porters to inland kingdoms and to markets on the Gulf of Guinea.

The trans-Sahara traffic was supplemented, beginning in the 15th Century, by European sailing ships. Portuguese caravels carried the bulk of the merchandise, sailing south around the great bulge of Africa to Axim and Elmina.

The products of the southern hinterland—gold, ivory and precious stones—were assembled at such inland citadels as Zimbabwe and carried by porters through thick forests to Sofala and other east coast seaports. From these smaller towns, dhows ferried the rich cargoes to the wealthy coastal island states of Kilwa and Lamu, the clearinghouses for nearly all the East African trade. Some of the products, such as gold, ivory and leopard skins, were shipped through the Red Sea to Kosseir in Egypt, and thence to Europe; the remainder awaited the favorable winds that would drive larger sailing vessels to India and China. The boats returned with porcelain, spices and cloth, some of which were shipped on to purchasers in Europe.

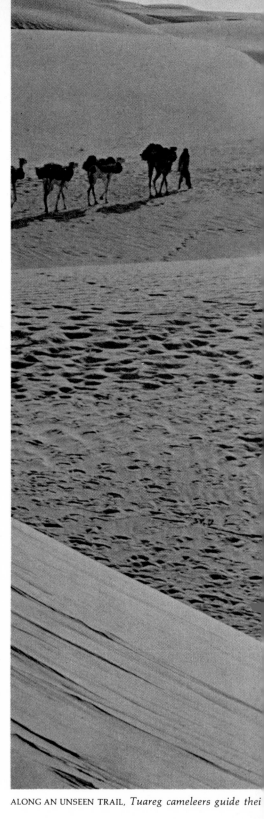

A SUN-BAKED OASIS *with a spring nearby, Djanet, in Algeria, has served caravans for centuries.*   ALONG AN UNSEEN TRAIL, *Tuareg cameleers guide thei*

THE SCORCHING TREK ACROSS THE SANDS

For centuries the lucrative West African trade routes have depended on the camel caravan. Without the camel the barren expanses of the Sahara would have effectively blocked contact between the fertile northern coast land and the rich forests of the south.

At the inland "ports" small groups with common destina-

...medaries across the Sahara. There are few landmarks, and the Tuaregs, like their ancestors, navigate by sun, stars and wind patterns in the sand.

tions would form caravans—sometimes as many as 12,000 camels strong—as protection from bandits. Then the caravans began their journeys, which lasted as long as three months, with only a few stops for water at oases along the way.

Though vital to trade, caravans were not a very efficient means of transport, largely because of the camels themselves.

Ill-tempered, surly beasts, they balked at every attempt to bridle or load them, biting or spitting at the cameleers. Even though hobbled at night, camels might wander three or four miles, causing a day's delay while they were rounded up. And once on the move the caravan could not stop until evening, for the camels would sit, spilling their loads onto the sand.

GUARDING THE COAST, *a minaret rises above Lamu Island, off present-day Kenya. On this island was located one of Africa's principal markets for ivory, and for mangrove-wood poles, widely used in house construction.*

FAIR WINDS TO THE EAST

While the traders of West Africa endured the sere desert and mosquito-ridden forest, those on the east coast had a relatively easy time. Blessed with a comfortable climate and good sailing winds, dhows *(right)* plied the coastal waters between the southern tip of Africa and the Red Sea, carrying cargoes of honey and coconuts, ivory and gold. Larger boats crossed the Indian Ocean, driven by the monsoons—winds that blow out of the west for half the year, the east for the other six months.

While this busy and profitable trade enriched many towns, its center was on the island of Kilwa, in what is now Tanzania. Kilwa's spacious harbor could accommodate the largest ships of the time, and the duties exacted from every vessel made its rulers among the wealthiest of the entire continent.

WORKHORSES OF TRADE, *dhows still sail Africa's coastal waters. Many are built today exactly as they have been for hundreds of years: of planks lashed together with strong, hand-braided fibers and caulked with pitch.*

EVAPORATION PITS *near Bilma, a major source of salt for some 500 years, are served by caravans of camels, which wait in the background to be loaded.*

SALT FROM THE DESERT

Salt was one of the most important commodities of the African trade, and was as common a medium of exchange as gold. The principal source of salt was the Sahara, where it was usually extracted by pouring water into hollows in saline earth. The water slowly leached out the salt, then evaporated in the sun, leaving a residue which was scooped out and packed into blocks. In some places like Taghaza, in Mali, the salt occurred in pure deposits and could be quarried. In this region, the 16th Century scholar Leo Africanus observed that the salt mines yielded a product "whiter than any marble."

SLABS OF SALT, *stacked by the hundreds, await shipment on the shores of Lake Chad. From this big lake on the southern border of the Sahara, boats carry the salt through inland waterways to southern settlements.*

IALE" AND "FEMALE" BASINS *dot Tegguida N'Tisemt in the cen-
l Sahara. Spring water, carried from large male pools (back-
ound) to smaller female basins, soaks up salt and evaporates.*

THE MARKET: GOAL OF ALL TRADERS

Whatever his product—and whether he carried it on camels, donkeys, dhows or on his porters' heads —the ultimate objective of the trader was the market place. There he put on his finest clothes, packed away during the long trip, and prepared to bargain for his due. In cities like Marrakech, the market area *(right)* was a sprawling section of town. With the first light of day the merchants and traders from every part of North Africa were in their allotted places and the area resounded with the shrill cries of traders hawking their wares and haggling over price. Was a bolt of cloth from Venice worth 30 ducats or only 25? Was a camel worth the salt it could carry, or only half a load? How much to pay for a horse from Europe, 40 ducats or 50? Only after such questions had been settled and all transactions made could the merchant turn homeward, to start once more on his cycle of trade.

ARGUING OVER GRAIN, *traders and farmers discuss prices in the market at Marrakech. Their language, costumes and techniques of barter are essentially the same today as they were hundreds of years ago.*

BIDDING FOR ANIMALS, *herdsmen and merchants jam the animal market at Goulimine, in Morocco. Here caravan leaders bicker over camels, while others restock their herds with cattle, goats and sheep.*

5
FOREST KINGDOMS

When the Portuguese first began to push south along the unknown coast of Africa, they encountered what they assumed to be isolated villages, and took what they wanted by raiding and piracy. "And when our men had come near," runs a report on one early Portuguese expedition south of Morocco, in 1441, "they attacked [the villages] very lustily, shouting at the tops of their voices 'Portugal!' and 'Santiago!' the fright of which so abashed the enemy that it threw them all into disorder."

But these tactics were short-lived. The Portuguese soon perceived that the coastal villages had inland protectors, kingdoms whose names the Portuguese had never heard of but whose wealth and power were impossible to deny. Accordingly, they changed their attitude. Instead of fighting the Africans, they sought to make them trading partners and allies. The king of Portugal might call himself "Lord of Guinea," but this was done simply to discourage his European rivals. His "royal brothers" in Africa acknowledged no such dominion, nor did he ask them to. "Most powerful and excellent King of Kongo," wrote Manuel of Portugal in 1512, "We convey you greetings in that We much love and esteem you, and to whom We pray God that he grant a long life and health as you would yourself desire." To which Nzinga Mbemba, the King of Kongo, replied, addressing Manuel, as he did in most of his 22 letters to Lisbon, "Most high and powerful Prince and King my brother. . . ."

Such terms were more than empty formalities. The Portuguese were impressed by the trading opportunities they found along the African coast, but they were no less impressed by their African allies' military power. The King of the Woloff people, in western Senegal, "can put into the field an army of about 10,000 cavalry and 100,000 footmen," wrote one Portuguese ex-governor who had been stationed at Elmina, on the Gold Coast, while the King of Mali, in the Western Sudan, "has 20,000 cavalry and innumerable footmen." Even these undoubtedly inflated figures say something about the Portuguese reaction to their new partners in commerce.

But it was the majesty of another kingdom—and its capital city—that set the tone for political relations between Europe and Africa in the late 15th and 16th Centuries. The kingdom and the city were

A CHIEF OF BENIN, *arrayed in ceremonial robes, is seen outside his home before leaving for the annual festival given in honor of the Oba's, or King's, father. The decorative sword held by the chief is a symbol of his authority.*

both called Benin. Its coast was first discovered in the 1470s, but not until 1486 did a Portuguese envoy, João Affonso d'Aveiro, penetrate the interior. D'Aveiro attempted to establish diplomatic and trading ties, and in the same year samples of pepper from Benin were "presently . . . sent to Flanders and to other parts, and soon it fetched a great price and was held in high esteem." So say the royal records at Lisbon.

D'Aveiro's mission was so successful that the King of Benin became interested in sending an ambassador to Lisbon. The man chosen for the role was Ohen-Okun, "a man of good speech and natural wisdom," wrote one contemporary Portuguese chronicler. Ohen-Okun was a priest at the shrine of the god Olokun—appropriately, the local god of the ocean—and he journeyed safely to Portugal in 1486 or shortly after, returning with gifts for his King, as well as for himself and his wife. Thereafter, for more than 100 years, Portugal maintained diplomatic contacts with Benin, and friendship between the two countries deepened.

"The favor which the king of Benin accords us," wrote the Portuguese agent at Benin some 30 years after D'Aveiro's first visit, "is due to his love of your highness; and thus he pays us high honor and sets us . . . to dine with his son, and no part of his court is hidden from us but all the doors are open." It became common for Benin merchants to learn the rudiments of Portuguese, and one English trader who visited the kingdom in 1553 noted that the King "could speak the Portuguese tongue, and had learned it as a child."

Many things about their African business partners surprised the Europeans. They were astonished at the quantity and variety of the goods they had to offer, and at their shrewd business sense. Every year, "from the Senegal River where you meet the first Negroes, as far as Sierra Leone," wrote Duarte Pacheco Pereira in 1506, "traders took more than

3,500 slaves, many elephants' tusks, fine cotton stuffs, and numerous other products." Furthermore, the trade was well ordered. If a European offended an African's sense of business propriety, the African might respond with boycotts and other stiff reprisals. The theft of a "muske cat" by one of the crew of an English merchantman in 1555 halted trade until restitution was made. "These Africans," the captain warned, "are very wary people in their bargaining," and anyone dealing with them "must use them gently, for they will not traffic or bring in any wares if they are badly treated."

The Africans were also quick to exploit the rivalries among their new partners. It soon became apparent to them that the European traders, however much they might look alike, were not united. The memoirs of an English sea captain in the African trade mention an all too typical encounter. On the 23rd of March, 1557, returning from a voyage to the coast of Guinea, Captain Towerson sighted "a ship in the weather of us, a Frenchman of 90 tons, who . . . coming near us, perceived that we had been upon a long voyage, and judging us to be weak . . . thought to have laid us aboard. . . . Whereupon we sent them some of our stuff, crossbars, and chainshots and arrows, so thick that it made the upper work of their ship fly about their ears."

Seeing in these rivalries a means of countering any one European power's attempts to monopolize trade, the Africans sought to make allies of them all. They played off the English and French against the Portuguese, and the Dutch against all three. But they also used these alliances to further their own internal ambitions. According to the logbook of the *Jesus*, an English privateer in the command of Captain John Hawkins, two African Kings sent emissaries to Hawkins while he was anchored in one of the estuaries of Sierra Leone in 1562. They asked him for military aid against two other Kings and promised in return to give Hawkins some of

A CORONATION CEREMONY in 1725 at Ouidah, on the Guinea coast, is shown in this drawing of the king (center) receiving homage. The presence of foreign guests indicates the special relationship of the Ouidah kings and their European partners. Of the rulers of Ouidah it was said, "They are so diligent in the slave trade that they . . . deliver a thousand every month."

their prisoners of war. Hawkins agreed, and was duly rewarded with 260 captives, whom he carried off to the West Indies in one of the earliest English sorties into the slaving trade.

From the logbooks of ships like the *Jesus* it is also apparent that the African peoples living along the Guinea coast and inland, in the rain forest, had a political life as advanced as that of their neighbors to the north, in the grasslands of the Western Sudan. "I saw and did eat and drink with six of their Kings or Mansas," wrote Richard Jobson in the early 17th Century, and added that these Kings had "reference to greater Kings living further inland. . . ." But the two regions differed in several ways. One of them was Islam. Spreading southward from North Africa in the Ninth through 11th Centuries, Muslim influence had brought the techniques of literacy, currency and credit, and civil bureaucracy to states in the Western Sudan, profoundly affecting the course of development of the great Sudanese empires. But nothing of the sort had happened farther south. Except for the occasional appearance of an itinerant Muslim merchant, Islam did not penetrate the forest and coastal kingdoms until the 16th Century. Literacy, in fact, did not arrive there until the first Europeans brought it with them. Nevertheless, 100 years before the Portuguese arrived, coastal Africa had achieved a certain maturity.

Two of the most creative of the wholly African coastal societies centered at the cities of Ife and Benin. According to legend, the peoples of Ife came from the Western Sudan, and may even have had some connection with the ancient metalworking land of Kush. Whatever their antecedents, by 1200 (according to the best archeological guess) the sculptors of Ife were producing superbly beautiful bronze heads and figures in honor of their kings. Sometime in the next two centuries they transmitted their bronze-casting techniques to the people of Benin, whose capital city became the seat of a powerful kingdom in the 15th Century.

One of the most successful of Benin's rulers was Ewuare the Great, who occupied the throne from 1440 to 1473. Oral histories say that he was a skilled magician, a doctor, a warrior, a brave and wise man. He is said to have enclosed 201 towns and villages within his spreading power and to have made Benin a famous city. It was Ewuare's Benin that the Portuguese discovered. But it is from the Dutch, who arrived there in the 17th Century, that the best descriptions of the city come. With their talent for precise detail, the Dutch traders set down the first factual reports of conditions along the Guinea coast.

In 1602 Amsterdam businessmen were able to buy a *Description of Guinea* compiled by Pieter de Marees from the accounts of many travelers. Among them was the observant D.R., probably Dierick Ruyters, who sojourned briefly in Benin under the rule of a king named Ehengbuda. The city, he wrote, was "very great when you go into it [for] you enter a great broad street, not paved, which seems to be seven or eight times broader than the Warmoes street in Amsterdam; it goes straight in and never bends." His lodgings, Ruyters said, were "at least a quarter of an hour's going from the gate, and yet I could still not see to the end of the street." Furthermore, many additional great streets opened from this main street, and they too were long: "You cannot see to the end of them because of their great length."

The houses along these streets, Ruyters continued, "stand in good order, one close and even beside the other as the houses in Holland stand. Those belonging to men of quality and others have two or three steps to go up, and along the front of them there is a kind of gallery where you may sit in the dry." The king lived in a collection of houses that were the largest of all: "The king's court is very big, having within it many wide squares with galleries round them where watch is always kept. I went so far within these buildings that I passed through four such squares, and wherever I looked I still saw gate after gate which opened into other places."

Sixty years later another Dutchman, Olfert Dapper, compiled a second collection of writings on Africa, drawing especially upon the reports of a certain Samuel Blomert. They confirm and extend Ruyters' observation. The king's palace, wrote Dapper, was a complex of buildings which "occupies as much space as the town of Haarlem and is enclosed within walls. There are numerous apartments for the Prince's ministers, and fine galleries most of which are as big as those on the Exchange at Amsterdam. They are supported by wooden pillars encased with bronze, where their victories are depicted, and which are carefully kept very clean." These bronze plaques, later brought to Europe, were used as a form of mnemonics by the king's "court remembrancers," to help them reconstruct their stories of Benin's past. Today the plaques are a pictorial record of what went on in Benin during the 16th and 17th Centuries. There are scenes of court life, of royal hunting parties and ceremonial occasions; some plaques even mark the coming of the Portuguese, wearing their heavy armor and unsuitable woolen clothing.

"These Negroes," wrote Dapper of the inhabitants of Benin, "are much more civilized than others on this coast. They are people who have good laws and a well-organized police; who live on good terms with the Dutch and other foreigners who come to trade among them, and to whom they show a thousand marks of friendship." But any foreigner who wished to prosper had to be careful to deal only with official agents and observe all the forms of protocol. Benin's trade was under the control of the king, whose agents came down to the port "magnificently dressed, wearing necklaces of jasper or fine coral." Upon meeting the visitors, said Dapper, the agents would offer "greetings on behalf of their king, ask for news of Europe and of Holland, and distribute various fruits which the king sends with them." The Dutch would "reply to these compliments with others," interrupting themselves only "for drinking."

Not until the following day did they get down to business, but then they might "bargain as hard as they can, sometimes for whole months." What the Dutch chiefly bought from Benin were "striped cotton garments which are retailed on the Gold Coast, and blue cloths which are sold on the rivers of Gabon and Angola, jasper stones, leopard skins, pepper," and a few "female slaves, for they refuse to sell men." In return the Dutch sold Benin "cloth of red and silver, drinking vessels, all kinds of fine cottons, linen, red velvet, embroidered silk, coarse flannel; candied oranges, lemons and other green fruit; bracelets of brass, gilded mirrors, iron bars; and Indian cowries [shells] which serve as currency there."

This new commerce with Europe was naturally a powerful stimulus to West African economic life and, indirectly, to its political and social life as well. Just as the trans-Saharan trade of the Western Sudan and the Indian Ocean trade of East Africa had encouraged the formation of large political units and a more elaborate society in those regions, so trade with Europe encouraged the kingdoms of the coastal forests of West Africa to expand and become more affluent.

But there were already evidences of trouble amid these promising developments. If much material good resulted from the European presence, it also brought one evil, the slave trade. In 1526 Nzinga Mbemba, the same King of Kongo who had such excellent relations with Portugal's King Manuel, had occasion to write Manuel's successor, John III, in quite another vein. He deplored the "excessive freedom given by your agents and officials to the men and merchants who are allowed to come here." Daily these merchants "seize upon our subjects, sons. of the land and sons of our noblemen and vassals and relatives . . . and cause them to be sold; and so great, Sir, is their corruption and licentiousness that our country is being utterly depopulated." By 1680 the Portuguese historian Cadornega could reckon that in the preceding century his fellow countrymen had enslaved "almost one million souls" from the western Congo and northern Angola. And Portugal, of course, was not alone in the enterprise.

To be sure, the African slave trade was not altogether a European innovation. Some form of slavery had existed in Africa, among Africans, for centuries. Prisoners of war and convicted criminals

NOT ONLY IN AFRICA

Africa, long thought of by Europeans as a breeding ground for the occult, was more than matched by Europe, with its own manias for alchemy, astrology and witch-burning. In the 15th Century, superstitious parishioners often danced among the graves in churchyards (above) in hopes of protecting themselves from the plague —while the skulls of plague victims peered quizzically at them. During the same period, Germany was burning an average of two witches a day.

Europeans, moreover, were constantly duped by promises of miraculous transformations and cures. Elixirs of life, magnets to attract diseases from the body, magic potions and healing fragments of the "true Cross" were common. Even such prominent intellectuals as Thomas Aquinas and Roger Bacon searched relentlessly for the philosopher's stone, the mystical charm of alchemy supposed to transform dross into gold. Yet despite all their delusions, Europeans thought of themselves as paragons of dignity and sensibility— while regarding faraway Africans as frightened primitives and painted witch doctors.

AN ASHANTI WARRIOR, *astride an elongated horse, is depicted in a figurine used as a counterweight on Ghana's Gold Coast. Objects such as this, cast in brass, copper or bronze, were placed on scales to measure out exact amounts of gold, the currency of local trade.*

were often treated as "wageless labor," liable to be bought and sold. However, there was one important distinction. They were not chattels as they came to be in the mines and plantations of the Americas. In African society there was no clear and rigid division between bond and free. Every African was a working member of some domestic group, attached normally through the bond of kinship. The slave, too, was a working member of a group, but since he was not kin, his status was lower. It need not, however, remain so. A slave could advance through work; he could buy his freedom with the produce of the plot of land assigned to him for cultivation. Or he could advance through good fortune, by inheriting goods or marrying his master's daughter. Through such means it was not at all unusual for slaves to acquire positions of great influence and power.

But in many cases it was this reservoir of "captive labor" within African society that opened the gates to overseas slavery. African chiefs and kings sold their slaves to Europeans just as they had always sold them to one another. In this respect,

moreover, they were behaving no differently from people in other cultures. For centuries the strong people in Europe had bought and sold their weaker brethren: even during the comparatively enlightened Renaissance, the pope more than once had occasion to excommunicate Venetian and Genoese merchants for selling Christian captives into Muslim slavery in Egypt and the Middle East.

If the African slave trade had never advanced beyond the immediate domestic needs of Africa and Europe, it might never have gotten out of hand. As things turned out, however, only nine years after Columbus' first trip across the Atlantic the Spanish throne issued a proclamation legalizing the import of slaves to its colonies in the Americas. Very soon, the African slave trade was transformed into a major element in the commerce of the Western world. Appalling numbers of human beings were thrust into foul and leaking ships, and the attitudes of men in the slave trade rapidly conformed to the essential cruelty of the business. Just as enterprising Europeans saw nothing wrong in buying captive humans for transportation across the seas, so it soon appeared right to the powerful men of Africa to sell them for this purpose. The few African rulers like Nzinga Mbemba who tried to interfere with the process were not strong enough to be effective and were quickly thrust aside.

Out of this grim but profitable business, new political units came into being. The city-states of the Niger delta, formerly nothing but fishing villages, grew prosperous and formed themselves into a highly organized trading network based almost wholly on the export of men and women brought downriver from the inner regions of the Niger basin. Even as late as the 1820s, when the slave trade was finally coming to a stop, the delta states were still shipping out approximately 20,000 people a year. Needless to say, this new prosperity along the coast was often gained at the cost of economic suffering in older, inland societies. The acquisition of European goods came to depend on a never-ceasing supply of captives, forcing states into continual acts of aggression and violence against one another—acts that after 1700 were likely to be carried out with European firearms. Many communities were grossly persecuted and some were utterly destroyed, while others, in order to avoid the slave raiders, migrated far from their ancestral homes. Even the winners eventually lost, for slavery gave Europe a foothold in Africa and thereby prepared the way for European colonial invasion.

And yet the damage (except in humanitarian terms) can be put too high. Some African states within the slave-trading region were scarcely disturbed by it at all. One of these was the remarkable kingdom of the Ashanti, which included after 1800 more than half of modern Ghana and parts of the neighboring states of the Ivory Coast and Togo. The Ashanti kingdom was by far the most successful of all the late kingdoms of precolonial Africa. Initially the Ashanti had built their strength on gold trade with the Western Sudan: they were one of the sources of the gold that moved north through the Sudanese trading empires to North African markets. Not for nothing was the office of their kings symbolized by a golden stool that, in Ashanti tradition, "came down from Heaven" and alighted gently on the knees of their hero-founder Osei Tutu in about 1695.

The Ashanti took the slave trade in their stride. They looked upon the presence of European merchants along the coast simply as a fresh source of commerce and a new means of strengthening their political power—one of these new means being muskets from faraway Birmingham. Never dominated by the pressures of European demands, the Ashanti skillfully played off the Dutch against the English and developed an efficient slave-trading organization of their own. It was run by a bureaucracy of literate clerks, and it commanded armies that no neighboring power could match. The Ashanti capital of Kumasi was the heart of a complex and profitable economic empire. Europeans, who first saw it in the early 19th Century, were impressed by its wide streets, clean houses and sanitary facilities that included such things as built-in plumbing.

They were also impressed by the abundant evidence of Ashanti power. Thomas Bowdich, who entered Kumasi in 1817 as the secretary of a British trading company, wrote that the company was greeted with great ceremony: "More than a hundred bands burst [forth] at once on our arrival, with the peculiar airs of their several chiefs; the horns flourished their defiances, with the beating of innumerable drums and metal instruments, and then yielded for awhile to the soft breathings of their long flutes. . . . At least a hundred large umbrellas, or canopies, which could shelter thirty persons, were sprung up and down by the bearers with brilliant effect, being made of . . . the most showy cloths and silks, and crowned on the top with crescents, pelicans, elephants" and other gold symbols, with valances "fantastically scalloped and fringed."

"Upwards of 5,000 people, the greater part warriors," met Bowdich and his company "with awful bursts of martial music . . . and a confusion of flags, English, Dutch and Danish." In all this the chiefs and captains moved with superb effect, wearing shimmering robes "of an incredible size and weight . . . thrown over the shoulder exactly like the Roman toga." On their feet were sandals of "green, red and delicate white leather." The King was "majestic yet courteous," displaying the "composure of a monarch"; he was seated on "a low chair richly ornamented with gold." Later the British were received in the royal palace, and Bowdich admired its "lofty and regular" architecture.

Bowdich may have let his pen run away with him a little, but his picture is essentially true. Other visitors to Kumasi in the 19th Century noted other evidences of Ashanti's political power. It did indeed have its own civil service, a bureaucracy staffed by Muslim and African clerks. It also had an unusually good courier system connecting all parts of the empire. "By day and night, the king's orders are despatched in all directions," wrote a Frenchman in the service of the Ashanti King in 1870. And its excellent army had a German drillmaster to train recruits. When finally overwhelmed by the British in 1901, after a devastating colonial war, the Ashanti had one foot in the modern world.

In this they were by no means alone. Although most of 19th Century Africa was far behind Europe in industry and technology, here and there a revolution was underway. The dynamic little Niger delta city-states, for instance, turned vigorously from the dwindling slave trade to what became known as "legitimate trade," and were soon deeply involved in the production and marketing of palm oil, an essential ingredient in soap. And the rulers of two of these delta states proved themselves to be the match of European traders in the struggle for industrial monopoly. Indeed, King Pepple of Bonny and King Ja Ja of Opobo were so skillful at outmaneuvering the Europeans that, all things being equal, they might very well have conquered the competition completely. But all things were not equal. By 1885 Britain had seized control of their two countries, and Pepple and Ja Ja ended their careers in British captivity.

Given a chance, perhaps other, older African societies might also have met the challenge of changing times as successfully as the youthful delta states. Certainly, most of them tried. When they failed, it was usually because the problems were too great, too puzzling for their venerable and traditional ways of doing things. Either they did not have the strength to control the conditions of change or they did not have the flexibility to adapt to them. Thus the once-powerful kingdom of Benin perished in a flood of human sacrifice as its kings and priests sought to ward off economic bankruptcy in the only way they knew how—by appeasing their gods. And the old Yoruba kingdom of Oyo, attacked by its neighbors and weakened by internal strife, had almost no resources to call upon and was an easy mark for colonial invasion.

In fact, over much of Africa the 19th Century was a time of unprecedented turmoil and violence. Instead of being allowed to work out its own relations with the modern world, Africa was shattered by the impact of foreign partition. It was an experience from which the majority of its peoples are only now beginning to recover. Through it all, while the fabric of his society fell apart, the individual African survived, drawing strength for this task from the long experience at disciplining himself to the demands of his environment—but even more, drawing strength from moral and spiritual beliefs of great antiquity and power. Today this spiritual heritage may be seen at work in a new context, as Africans seek to transform a continent.

ROYAL SENTRIES *and fanbearers guard the Oba's palace; the serpent on the roof symbolizes his power.*

THE METROPOLIS OF BENIN

Long before Europeans set foot in tropical Africa, the powerful nation of Benin was thriving in what is now southern Nigeria. A dignified and law-abiding people, the Bini paid proud obeisance to their king, or Oba, who ruled through a well-ordered hierarchy of counselors and local governors. The capital city, also called Benin, is today only a small provincial town, but for centuries it was one of the most important commercial and cultural centers of western Africa.

Since the Bini had no written language, the only detailed descriptions of life in Benin are in the journals of early European explorers. The Bini did, however, leave an eloquent record of their civilization in bronze plaques commissioned by the Oba to adorn the pillars of his palace *(above)*. These remarkable reliefs show the Bini as vigorous and very human members of a uniquely African culture.

A RESPLENDENT MONARCH, *the Oba (second from right) is flanked by chieftains and protected by heavily armed royal guards (left). His oversized neckla*

...ar hammer, anklets and ornamented kilt are all symbols of his majestic power.

THE QUEEN MOTHER, *who groomed the Oba's heir for kingship, lived with her handmaidens and bodyguards a few miles from Benin—far enough away to keep her from meddling in politics.*

THE AWESOME POWER OF BENIN'S KING

The Oba of Benin was an absolute monarch who could command anything he wished with the knowledge that he would be instantly obeyed. The actual business of governing was left to his counselors, who directed military, economic and agricultural matters in the Oba's name. This state of affairs was probably agreeable to the Oba, whose time was taken up by countless ceremonies and sacrifices, and by his harem of a hundred or more wives.

But in spiritual matters the Oba was paramount. Not only was he the earthly representative of all Benin's gods, but he was himself godlike; anyone who believed otherwise was executed as a heretic.

A ROYAL HOLIDAY IN BENIN

At least once a month the citizens of Benin put aside their work and embarked on a day or more of exuberant festivities. The nobles gathered in the Oba's court, where they would sip bamboo wine, dance, play games, chew kola nuts and frolic with the women of the court.

The high points of these celebrations generally were the sacrificial executions of slaves or convicted felons. Accounts of religion in Benin are vague, but the Bini apparently believed in a supreme god who created and ruled the earth; they considered it useless to worship him, however, since he was already benevolent. Instead, they worshiped numerous lesser gods, who they felt could mediate for them with the supreme god. The human sacrifices were offered not to the gods, but to the devil, whom the Bini blamed for all their misfortunes. Victims rarely struggled; some actually assisted the executioner, and a few even volunteered to be sacrificed —powerful proof of the intensity of their religion.

CAMOUFLAGED *in large, bushy helmets, hunters warily stalk a leopard. When they finally cornered their prey, they often proved their courage by captur-*

HUNTING: AN ELITE PROFESSION

Among the most prestigious citizens in Benin were the hunters, a group of rugged professionals who were the envy of the kingdom. Only the most exceptional boys could become hunters, and then only after completing a rigorous apprenticeship. They had to learn how to track game in every type of terrain, how to move swiftly and silently through the thorny underbrush, how to survive in the forest for days without food.

alive and bringing it back to the Oba's court.   A STEALTHY ARCHER, *an arrow fitted to his bow, takes aim at a plump ibis on a branch above him.*

They also had to memorize a whole catechism of secret rituals, such as the ceremony that was supposed to make a hunter invisible to his prey.

If a boy proved to be an outstanding student, he might be fortunate enough to become not only a hunter, but an elephant hunter. Armed with blowguns and poisoned darts, elephant hunters were a special, almost legendary, class. Their work was exceedingly dangerous. The poison, though lethal, worked slowly; their frenzied victim might go crashing blindly through the forest for several days before it finally died. One of the elephant's tusks went to the Oba; the man responsible for the kill received the other—along with the head, heart and lungs, which were considered to be powerful talismans that assured him of even greater success on his next venture.

A NATION OF TRADERS

When the first Europeans arrived, Benin was already a bustling commercial center that conducted large-scale trade throughout western Africa. Bini merchants dealt in ironwork, weapons, farm tools, wood carvings and foodstuffs ranging from yams to dried lizards. And since Benin had mastered the concept of money, transactions were not restricted to simple bartering. The currency consisted of cowrie shells and metal rings called manillas.

Early European traders, expecting easy pickings, were surprised when they found what shrewd businessmen they were dealing with. One trader complained that "we have generally to wait eight or ten days before we can agree upon a price with them."

AN ELEGANT RIDER *arrives from the north. His feathered headdress suggests that he may be a bodyguard of an emir from northern Nigeria who sometimes traveled to Benin on important business.*

CHIEF OF PROTOCOL, *the Royal Greeter officially welcomed merchants and distinguished visitors to the Oba's court.*

A MASTER MERCHANT *(right) w licensed by the Oba to deal wi Europeans, an honor accorded on to the craftiest traders. The cre cent in his left hand is a manil Benin's most valuable money un*

A FIERCE WARRIOR *gets set to hurl his spear. His ornamented shield of thin bamboo was little protection against a direct spear thrust, but it probably could ward off glancing blows. His highly decorative kilt was made of fibers spun to the texture of fine silk.*

TRIUMPHANT IN BATTLE *elaborately armored Bini swordsmen lead a prisoner of war (immediate right) back to Benin as a slave. Such soldiers, early explorers reported, were highly disciplined, and would not yield a step even when they were in imminent danger of death.*

WARFARE, DECLINE AND FALL

War was a constant of life in Benin; according to some accounts the nation could mobilize 100,000 warriors in a day. The object of their fighting was territorial expansion and the acquisition of booty and slaves.

After the Europeans arrived, the slave trade mushroomed; farming and commerce were slighted and the economy—inevitably—started to collapse. The Oba, believing his bad fortune was the work of the devil, ordered more and more human sacrifices to turn the tide. But by 1897 the disintegration was complete; that year a British force found the city of Benin all but deserted and littered with the bodies of sacrificial victims. After four centuries of greatness, Benin had finally passed into history.

6

GODS AND SPIRITS

A middle-aged African carrying three spears and a wooden bowl comes down a forest path and stops before a doorway in a brown clay wall. Tall trees climb on every hand, but the tallest is a giant cottonwood rising from within the walled compound. The African pauses at the door, leans his spears respectfully against the lintel and steps within. He is there to consult the Priestess of the Python, and his bowl contains an offering of mashed plantains and kola nuts, hot from the heat of his nervous hands, for visiting a priestess can be an anxious business. Lansana is a skilled metalsmith, and he has come to the priestess because he is worried; last week two of his little beehive furnaces collapsed for no reason he can understand, and two valuable smeltings were ruined.

Lansana's story is a contemporary one, but it would have been essentially the same 100 years ago, and very probably even long before that. Nowhere is Africa's traditionalism more apparent than in its religions. Although Islam and Christianity have coexisted with them for centuries, and have enormously influenced Africa, the old religions are still used for practical problems by practical-minded men like Lansana. Given a mystery, he prefers to find an answer through the tried and proven methods of his ancestors. The priestess and her kind administer those methods, and in a curious way their ministrations work.

As Lansana speaks to the priestess of the damage to his furnace and smeltings, with its hint of hidden evil, of witch-made malice by a person or persons unknown, Lansana becomes excited. But the priestess remains calm. She asks questions, endless questions, and says nothing. When she has no more questions she goes to the silver-gray roots of the cottonwood tree, stoops and picks up something. It is a beautiful snake, slender and shining in the sun. She places it before an altar of enchanted stones while Lansana waits, hoping for the best, the noonday heat beating upon his bare head. The python gives no sign of life except for a faint pulsing beneath the golden skin of its throat.

A long time passes. At last the priestess turns to Lansana with her answers. He has offended the ancestors by too much haste for wealth, has been remiss in his social duties, has behaved meanly to

his cousin Camara. Let him sacrifice a goat and make amends to Camara, let him give help where help is due, and once again the ancestors will afford him their protection. Lansana listens and is annoyed, but at the same time his worries drop away from him, for the mystery of the smeltings is solved.

Lansana's priestess and her python exist in innumerable variations all over the African continent, performing the local equivalents of this same function. They are the very bedrock of an ancient and elaborate set of religious beliefs that permeate African life. But what sort of religious ideas and beliefs can be expressed in such terms? Were they, as one 17th Century missionary called them, "hellish delusions"? Were they blind and pointless superstitions, crude and childish make-believe? Were Africans simply fetish worshipers, idolaters of magical lumps of wood and stone? All these and many similar labels were pinned on Africans by non-Africans—sometimes with unconscious irony ("fetish" comes from the Portuguese *feitiço*, a magic talisman worn by Portuguese sailors as protection against evil spirits). More thoughtful men, armed with the findings of modern research, see things otherwise.

African religion, in the words of anthropologist William Howells, is "a godly religion of a most general kind." Its gods have attributes that are more or less human, and offer their worshipers the kind of sympathy and protection common to many other religions. Africans evidently thought about God in ways deserving of respect from the very earliest time of their dispersal across the continent. Religion, in fact, can be said to have been the regulating force in all they said and did. Like Christians of the Middle Ages, pagan Africans lived in an age of faith. *Ex ecclesiam non est vita*, "there is no life outside the Church," runs the Christian maxim— and so might it run for Africa. The priestess and

A NAIL FETISH, *this wooden dog was used to invoke magical powers for good luck. When a merchant wanted special profits, or a warrior wished invulnerability in battle, or a woman sought painless childbirth, a nail was driven into a figure such as this one.*

her kind were not mumbo jumbo, but elements in a rounded and efficacious system of moral and spiritual teaching, without which the Africans could never have built and maintained their stable societies, their patterns of law and order, their standards of good and bad, their measures for bringing comfort to the sick and relief to the troubled and despairing.

African religion achieved these ends in widely different ways—in almost as many ways as there were African peoples. As each migrant group splintered away from its parent tribe, moving out in search of new land, it carried its old beliefs along, gradually modifying and changing them to suit its new conditions of life. Thus people living in the rain forests of the Congo, scarcely ever seeing the sky, came to have very different ideas about the origin and operation of the world from people living in the sky-enclosing plains of the open grasslands. And people whose homes lay within sound of the Atlantic surf developed different religious needs from people living inland, along the banks of rivers. But however varied the particulars of their beliefs and practices, African religions shared many similar ideas about the supernatural world.

Nearly all Africans believed in a single High God from whom all things flowed. He was seldom regarded as human in form, but rather as the Energy that differentiated life from matter, a sort of Life-Force. From this conviction about a Life-Force, Africans drew certain conclusions about the nature of man. One of these was that the dead do not really die. They leave the earth to rejoin the Life-Force, but at the same time they retain a spiritual identity. And since no one dies, in the sense of being utterly abolished, every community of the living also includes the spirits of its dead. More than that, it also includes the spirits of those not yet born. An African chief once explained to a British commission of inquiry into West African customs that he thought of the land as belonging to "a vast family, of which many are dead, few are living, and countless members are unborn."

The High God, most Africans also believed, once lived down among men, and the explanations for why he left are strikingly similar. The Dinka, in the Sudan, and the Ashanti, far to the west in Ghana, both say that the cause was women. God,

A MOUSE ORACLE, *in the form of a small urn guarded by a human figure, was one of the more esoteric devices used by Baule diviners of the Ivory Coast. Sticks were carefully arranged inside the jar and then mice placed in it. By reading the new patterns of sticks produced by the moving animals, a diviner told fortunes, settled disputes, identified witches and thieves, and even located lost articles. Diviners were frequently consulted by clients needing personal or business guidance.*

say the Dinka, withdrew from man because one day a deplorably greedy woman, wanting more than her fair share of land, hit God with her hoe. Forthwith, God sent a small, blue bird, a bird as blue as the sky of the Sudan, to cut the rope that had always given people a link with heaven. In Ashanti they say that God left man because an old woman repeatedly jolted him with her pounding stick while she was making fufu (a dish of mashed plantains or yams). "Then one day God said, 'Because of what you are doing to me, I am taking myself far up into the sky where men cannot reach me.' And of a truth he did."

For the most part this High God played only an indirect role in man's affairs. Beneath him was a host of lesser gods who acted as intermediaries and also presided over the physical workings of the universe—gods of storm, of mountains, of thunder, rivers, snakes, seas, trees, iron. Olodumare, the High God of the Yoruba of Nigeria, for example, made the earth but did not do any of the actual work. In fact, he made it in four days, setting aside the fifth as a day of rest and worship—a work week

happily suited to the climate of the tropics. But the real labor was performed by a lesser god, Orishanla, who scattered earth over the watery waste, planted trees and later created human bodies into which Olodumare breathed life. (With a typical touch of village practicality, Olodumare sent along a sacred chameleon to check on how well Orishanla was carrying out his orders.)

Most of these lesser gods were local gods, sacred to one community, and each community evolved what might be called its own "spiritual charter" with the supernatural—its own particular form of spiritual reassurance and identity. For a long time the nature of these charters was hidden from the outside eye by the simplicity and crudity of the religious equipment. Africans built no monumental churches and seldom bothered with the panoply of priestly garb. Their temples and shrines were humble affairs, often containing an altar that was no more than a lump of wood or piece of stone, and were frequently littered with a collection of pots and other everyday objects. And yet these shrines and altars, seemingly so makeshift and

AFRICAN MAGIC CHARMS

Threatened by unknown forces, and sometimes by hunger and beasts of prey, Africans, like other peoples, enlisted the aid of magic. Their techniques were largely pragmatic and derived from everyday experience; for example, if a farmer plucked a round black stone from a river bed and was thereafter blessed by several good crops, in time he was likely to consider round black stones standard insurance for good crops. Similarly, the teeth of dreaded lions and crocodiles were regarded as powerful medicine against wild beasts—particularly if a hunter wore them and returned successfully from the hunt. Objects that did not work were discarded; those that did were widely copied, and gradually became standardized and stylized into symbolic magical devices. African scholars have classified many of these devices into talismans, or general good luck charms, and amulets, used to ward off specific evils. In practice, however, eclectic Africans used magical objects less by category than by what they actually seemed to do. Following are some of the most common African charms, and their uses·

PIECES OF STRAW	Protect crops from harm
PALM-FROND ARCHWAYS	Shield villages from disease
BUNDLES OF FEATHERS	Guard occupants of a room
RAFFIA BROOMS	Keep away burglars
ANIMAL CARVINGS	Ensure a good hunt
ANIMAL TEETH	Keep off wild animals
IRON BRACELETS	Promote fertility
BUNDLES OF STICKS	Guard the home
BAMBOO WHISTLES	Defend against witchcraft
GOATSKIN POUCHES	Ward off illness
CHEWING STICKS	Prevent quarrels
HEAVY ANKLETS	Protect weak children
TWISTED COPPER RINGS	Prevent snake bites

casual, were revered and even dignified places of worship—made so by the sincerity of the worshipers' beliefs. They were sacred places where men and women could come to consult their oracles and pray to their gods—behind their simplicity lay complex systems of spiritual homage and social conduct.

Because religious beliefs and practices played so large a part in African life, the custodians of the temples and shrines were people of great importance. No doubt they were as varied in their talents and characters as any such body of specialists would be. Yet if some were frauds and rascals, most were skillful practitioners in the arts of physical and mental healing. Their authority came partly from a broad knowledge of herbal medicine, plus psychological insight and an intimate understanding of local circumstances. But it also came from the general belief in the priest's or priestess' power to mediate with the spirit world. In Ashanti, for example, the shrine priest was called an *okomfo*, from *kom*, which means to prophesy or predict, and his main duty was to care for the sacred object through which he evoked the god. "This he does," wrote Robert Rattray, the British anthropologist, "by tinkling a bell, drumming, and, most important of all, by dancing. He will know when the spirit has taken up its abode in the body provided for it by being seized with tremblings and shakings. . . . The *okomfo* then addresses the spirit and gives its answers to those who have come to consult it. . . ."

Such skills required arduous training, and among some African peoples there was a regular course of schooling for shrine priests. In Ashanti, a novice studied for three years, during which time he was said to be "married" to the god. The first year he learned the ceremonial use of herbs—which leaves to rub on his ankles to strengthen them for dancing; which to rub on his eyes so that he could "see his god daily"; which to take in order to arouse the spirit of possession. During the second year he learned the laws and taboos of the god. He was told never to drink intoxicating liquors, never to gossip, never to quarrel or fight, never to call upon his god to kill anyone, never to attend the chief's court unless invited, never to go out at night to join other young men. In addition, he was always to salute his elders by bending his right knee and touching the ground with his right hand. Finally, in his last year, the priest-to-be learned the arts of divination and incantation and the proper forms of addressing his god.

The gods of Africa controlled the mysteries of nature; they were the spirits to whom one appealed for help and protection against the unknown. But when it came to mundane affairs, another set of religious beliefs came into play. These concerned the spirits of the ancestors, and the people in each community who were appointed to speak for them, for it was the ancestors who guaranteed the survival and prosperity of the communal group. They were the "founding fathers" who had laid down the good and safe path for each community to tread. It was they who had "first come into the country," as the Africans put it, and who had decided the community's religious, moral and social rules. If suitably served, the ancestors were powerful aids to a secure and prosperous life; if ignored or insulted, they were dangerous enemies.

But the relationship of the living to the dead was not simply one of awe and respect. There was also another element, in the nature of a contract or a bargain. The living owed a duty to the ancestors, but the ancestors owed one in return: each was expected to look after the interests of the other, and meticulous ceremonies and rituals were employed to honor and renew this contract. Consequently, a man did not worship all his ancestors indiscriminately, or even those for whom he might have a special, personal admiration or respect. He worshiped only those who were recognized as standing in the direct line of succession from some distant founder; only these authorized ancestors could act as intermediaries with the original ancestral spirit. In a way the "appointed ancestors" were not un-

like the canonized saints of the Christian church.

The worship of ancestors was one of the central organizing factors in African society. It regulated the lives of individuals, of villages, of groups of villages and of nations. The great Ashanti empire that arose in Ghana toward the close of the 17th Century rested on an agreement between the Ashanti peoples to unite their ancestors under a single symbol, the Golden Stool of Osei Tutu. But even at village level, ancestor cults assured law and order in a number of different ways: they were intimately connected with the traditional "rites of passage"—birth, puberty, marriage and burial—and they controlled the village economy through the agency of the "secret societies" that were the executors of the ancestral laws.

At puberty, along with the customary tests for bravery and maturity, a child was ritually introduced to his ancestors. He learned how they had founded his village with the help of the gods and how they had organized a way of life for themselves and their descendants. He was introduced to the masks and other cult objects associated with the ancestors and was told what they stood for. He learned that his own life would prosper only if he obeyed the ancestral will—observed the rules and regulations laid down by the ancestors, lived as they had lived, no worse but not much better.

At the end of this period of indoctrination, which sometimes lasted a number of weeks, the child was officially considered an adult and a member of his community's "secret society." These governing associations were secret only to the extent that none but members could attend their ceremonies. Otherwise, everyone was aware of them, and indeed had to be, for it was these societies of men (and sometimes women) who applied the ancestral laws, modified them when necessary and made sure they were carried out.

Some of these societies powerfully influenced

INITIATION MASKS, *topped by figures of beasts and birds, and fringed with bushy raffia collars, are donned by Bayaka boys in the Congo upon graduating to manhood. Their formal initiation into adult status is held when the boys return from a "bush school," where they have lived for weeks receiving instruction in secret rites and responsibilities to the tribe.*

Africa's early trade with Europe. Visiting mariners in the 15th Century found that they could neither buy nor sell goods along the Guinea coast without the approval of the elders who headed the Poro society. Like other such societies, the Poro was essentially religious. But the broad democracy of its membership, backed by the authority of ancestral sanctions, gave it a strong role in all the practical aspects of community life as well. The Poro existed to interpret the will of the ancestors, but it also arranged public festivals, settled secular disputes and set market prices for everything from yams to gold. Religion and politics thus went hand in hand.

For the individual African, however, religion did not end with prayer to the gods and respect for the ancestors. The supernatural made itself felt at a third level: in sorcery and witchcraft. Like Europeans before the age of scientific explanation, Africans believed in magic. There was good magic and bad; the former could be helpful, even benevolent, the latter disastrous, especially when it was the deliberate work of sorcerers. But evil could also come from the unpremeditated work of witches. These were malicious spirits who left the bodies of their human hosts and flew about at night on secret missions, just as they did in 16th and 17th Century Christian Europe. To deal with them—and, in fact, to deal with all forms of sorcery—Africans turned to a specialist in magic, commonly called a witch doctor. The real function of the witch doctor was to advise and protect people threatened by evil spirits, but occasionally a witch doctor would himself "go bad" and traffic in dangerous spells.

The force of such beliefs varied greatly. Some peoples, like the Zande of the southern Sudan, were obsessed by witchcraft and believed that witches influenced every facet of life; other peoples, like the Tallensi of Ghana, had no such apprehensions. But no matter how prevalent the fear of witches, few Africans believed that unusual occurrences were wholly supernatural; even the Zande distinguished between the act of bad magic and the cause of the act. A Zande bitten by a snake knew very well that it was the snake's poison that harmed him. What he did not know, and what he feared, was the reason for the snake's bite. Disbelieving in the accidental, he wanted to know why the snake had bitten him and not someone else, and who it was that willed the snake to be lying in his path.

To find out, the Zande consulted an oracle. Most often the oracular medium he used was a certain poison that, when fed to a chicken, might or might not prove fatal. While the poison was being administered the questioner ritually petitioned the oracle for an answer. Depending upon whether the chicken lived or died, the petition was granted or left in abeyance. Sometimes the cost of this consultation came high—a particularly worrisome problem could drive a troubled man to use a great many chickens.

Tests and ordeals that used herbal brews were also common practice in witch-doctoring. The famous Dr. David Livingstone noted that suspected African witches were given powerful emetics that they vomited if they were innocent and that purged them if they were guilty. The same technique, the Scottish doctor observed, had been used in his own country, in reverse. In Scotland, "the supposed witch, being bound hand and foot, was thrown into a pond; if she floated, she was considered guilty . . . if she sank and was drowned, she was pronounced innocent."

Witch-doctoring is written off in the modern world as arrant nonsense, but in traditional Africa the witch doctor served a real and useful purpose, quite aside from his magic. He was often able to settle disputes between rivals that might have led to violence, and his knowledge of the medicinal value of herbs frequently led him to prescribe remedies that actually cured. Also, through his intimate knowledge of the lives of the people in his community, and of human nature in general, it was not unusual for him to function as a sort of prescientific psychologist. When Lansana stepped through the door of the brown clay wall to consult the Priestess of the Python about his ruined smeltings, he was there for comfort and advice. And the priestess, from long acquaintance with Lansana as an individual, was able to provide them.

This faith in the healing qualities of African religion, in its physical and mental therapeutic powers, helps to explain why Islam and Christianity have never completely wiped out traditional African beliefs. But it is not the only explanation. In their way, African religions offered Africans an indigenous version of the concept of immortality. The worship of the ancestors, with its profound sense of tribal continuity, extended life beyond death. More than that, it gave the individual African a spiritual identity with a group whose pattern of life had never changed, as far back as the mind could remember.

Undoubtedly this is one main reason why the old Christian missionaries so often complained of backsliding among their African flocks, and why Islam, for all its tolerance of certain traditional African customs, was long resisted. For Africans the goal in life was to live as one's fathers had lived. It might not be progress, but it was stability. Thus, the force and dignity of African religion was not in its parts, but its whole. Men such as Lansana were embraced from cradle to grave by a system of beliefs and moral guides that had been evolved, however unconsciously, through centuries of trial and error. The system oiled the wheels of personal and community life and made them run smoothly; it was the very heart of all African societies. So well did it work that it lasted through all the turmoil of colonial times—and thus still serves Lansana today.

A SAINT IN STONE *on one of Lalibela's churches is inscribed St. George but may be Lalibela himself.*

CHURCHES HEWN FROM ROCK

In 1520 the Portuguese explorer and missionary Francisco Alvares penetrated the highlands of central Ethiopia and found himself in the midst of a nation of intensely pious Christians. Ethiopia, in fact, had been converted in 333 A.D., and for more than three centuries was in lively contact with Alexandria, the spiritual center of the faith in North Africa. But in 640 A.D. Egypt fell to Islam, and Ethiopia was cut off from the mainstream of Christianity for more than 800 years.

Alvares was doubly amazed when he saw the Ethiopians' places of worship, particularly the monolithic churches in Lalibela, a remote mountain village that once had been Ethiopia's capital. Ten of these churches had been carved from solid rock during the 13th Century under the direction of King Lalibela, who gave his name to the town. Unlike so many relics of ancient Africa, the churches are still very much alive: through the centuries Lalibela has become known as "the Jerusalem of Ethiopia," and pilgrims still travel hundreds of miles to worship there.

EWING STONE *with an adze, a workman (said to be Lalibela) completes a church.*

INISHED CHURCHES *are depicted as tall structures enclosed by a symbolic wall.*

THE LEGEND OF A HEAVENLY TASK

For centuries scholars have wondered what could have inspired King Lalibela to undertake the enormous task of carving 10 churches from solid rock. According to a 19th Century Ethiopian manuscript, three of whose illustrations are reproduced at left, God inspired Lalibela to build the churches; moreover, after Lalibela's subjects had finished each day's work, the angels pitched in at night.

Historians give a somewhat different account. Lalibela's ancestors, they say, had usurped the Ethiopian throne from the Solomonid dynasty about 1100 A.D. and begun the Zagwe dynasty. But the country under the Zagwes declined in power and prestige, and the Solomonids grew dangerously strong. Lalibela built the churches to give grandeur to his capital city, to overshadow the Solomonids and, most important, to gain the favor of Ethiopia's Christian clergy as the legitimate king.

However secular his motives may have been at first, Lalibela was a changed man by the time the work was done. According to legend he had spent all his wealth to finance the project. He slept on rocks, ate only herbs and roots and, when the last church was completed more than two decades later, abdicated the throne to lead a life of Christian contemplation. Today, though other Zagwe rulers are regarded by Ethiopians as unmitigated scoundrels, King Lalibela is revered as a true saint.

AINTHOOD *is promised by God (left) to Lalibela as a reward for his holy task.*

DEEP IN A HILLSIDE *of volcanic rock, the Church of St. George is reached by a narrow subterranean trench, visible as a dark rectangle at the left of the picture*

CONCENTRIC CROSSES *are carved into the church's roof, which is almost exactly level with the surface of the ground from which the pit around it was excavated*

A HIDDEN SANCTUARY

Nowhere in Lalibela is the enormity of the church-builders' task more vividly illustrated than in the Church of St. George, seen here. The workers chipped away at the bedrock until they had dug a trench 40 feet deep, leaving a huge block of stone, which they painstakingly carved into the shape of a Greek cross and then hollowed out.

A legend connected with the church states that it was built after St. George, who was furious that no church had been erected in his honor, galloped into town and ordered the workers to construct one. Supporting the tale is a stone near the church; clearly imprinted in it is a curious hooflike mark.

A STEPPED BASE *follows the massive contours of the church, widening out at the main entrance steps and at a door to a side chapel at the right.*

LALIBELA'S WINDOWS: A MEETING OF CULTURES

The architecture of the churches of Lalibela reflects the blending of a great many different cultural influences, as can be seen in the array of windows shown here. The Greek, Roman and Byzantine elements in the designs of some of the windows probably filtered into Ethiopia with Christian refugees from Muslim persecution in Egypt. One authority has claimed to have identified motifs from as far away as Persia, central Asia and China. This is entirely plausible: although Ethiopia was largely cut off from the Christian nations to the north of the Mediterranean, it had established strong commercial and cultural ties with the nations of the Middle East, which in turn were trading with the Orient.

POINTED WINDOWS *of Muslim origin appear abou Christian crosses on Abba Libanos. The church wa partially rebuilt of masonry after an earthquak*

SWASTIKA MOTIFS, *ancient mystical symbols common in Persia and the East, are interspersed with other kinds of crosses on the Church of St. Mary.*

A GREEK CROSS, *as elaborate as the gold altarpiec used by Lalibela's priests, reflects early contac with the Orthodox Church in the Mediterranea*

134

ROMANESQUE ARCHES *on the Church of St. Mascal rise above a window of swastikas and twinned crosses.*

A ROMAN CROSS *and two ornamental openings below it were probably inserted after this church was built.*

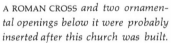

AN ORNATE FRAMEWORK, *in the wall of the Church of Golgotha, combines a pointed opening with a delicate, tendrillike tracery, all surmounted by a Maltese cross.*

ROCK-HEWN INTERIORS *illustrate the process used by the builders. Starting from one end of each aisle (center picture), they carved away bits of stone, slowly*

INTRICATE WORKMANSHIP
IN SOLID STONE

The extraordinary workmanship that went into the churches of Lalibela is strikingly evident in the arching vaults and decorated columns of their interiors. There are no records in existence to indicate all the tools the builders used, or what methods they followed to achieve such precision. It is con-

exposing columns and vaults to hold up the roof. Finally these were decorated with elaborate geometric designs such as the intertwined circles seen above.

ceivable that some of the workers were skilled artisans from Byzantium, or even from Rome. Even the great European architects of the period—who could build from the ground up with stones and mortar, bricks and beams, plumb lines and scaffolding—were scarcely achieving better results. The rock from which the churches of Lalibela were hewn is a red volcanic tuff common throughout the mountains of Ethiopia. This material is relatively easy to carve—but while European builders could correct their errors, in Lalibela a surveying miscalculation or a moment of carelessness might have ruined a whole church.

HEALED BY CHRIST, *a cripple picks up his bed and walks, as the Samaritan woman draws water for Christ (center). The inscriptions above are in Geez, the ancient language used in the Ethiopian liturgy.*

OLD TESTAMENT HEROES *Shadrach, Meshach and Abednego are seen as princely figures painted in a style influenced by Byzantine art, with eyes averted and a suggestion of mosaic in their crowns.*

SCENES FROM A RICH BIBLICAL HERITAGE

The walls of the Churches of St. Mary and St. Merkurios at Lalibela are resplendent with murals depicting Biblical episodes. Many of the scenes are from the Old Testament; Ethiopian history and folklore are intimately linked with Judaism, and the Ethiopians are themselves a mixture of Semitic, West Asian and Negroid strains.

Ethiopia's earliest Christian rulers, the kings of the Solomonid dynasty, claimed to be descended from King Menelik I, the firstborn son of King Solomon and Sheba, Queen of the ancient Ethiopians. Rulers of the Zagwe dynasty, including King Lalibela, went a step further—they traced their ancestry all the way back to Moses. But the Zagwe dynasty was overthrown by the Solomonids in 1270, and ever since then Ethiopia has been ruled by the descendants of Solomon—one of the longest uninterrupted lines of royal succession in history.

THE HOLY MYSTERIES
OF A SUBTERRANEAN CRYPT

The bedrock beneath Lalibela is honeycombed with mysterious passageways, tunnels and caves, many of which are used as burial vaults or as sacred places of worship. The most sacred of all is the Selassie (Trinity) Crypt above, in the deepest recesses of the Church of Golgotha-Mikael. Few outsiders

have ever been permitted to see it. In this ultimate sanctuary the priests of Lalibela celebrate the most solemn ceremonies in the Ethiopian liturgy.

The three structures are altars; the center one, the Altar of the Four Evangelists, depicts St. Matthew as an angel. The holes in the floor may have been used as receptacles for religious offerings, or they may have anchored posts that supported a canopy. In another part of the church there is a chamber that houses two notable tombs: King Lalibela is buried in one; the other is said by worshipers to be the tomb of Adam himself.

7
ARTS THAT
CAPTURE LIFE

Africa's traditional arts, like its beliefs and customs, were the product of an age of faith. Just as Europe during the Middle Ages built cathedrals and composed music to the glory of God, so Africa's artists were concerned mainly with the spiritual content of their work. In sculpture, in music, in dancing and in story they attempted to express and celebrate the moral and religious convictions that underlay their daily life. From this concern African art acquired two chief characteristics—variety in form and conventionality in style. The forms were varied because the beliefs and rituals of African religion were varied; the style was conventional because the art was meant to express ideas laid down by long-established precedent. In short, it was an art that was neither haphazard nor spontaneous.

But this is not how non-Africans generally looked upon it. The first African art to make an impact of any size on the outside world reached Paris just after the turn of the century. It consisted of ritual masks and figurines carved of wood, brought from French, Belgian and German holdings in equatorial Africa. Grotesque and often oddly proportioned, it was an art judged by artists and critics alike to be entirely free—the product of the emotion of the moment, shaped only by the sculptor's private vision. Here surely, the experts agreed, was the direct expression of individual feelings of fear, awe, anger, love and other elemental sensations. How else could one explain these contorted features, so urgently furious, so affecting, so difficult to understand within the context of familiar forms of art?

This judgment, made without sufficient knowledge of the background from which the masks and figures had come, led most Europeans astray. They labeled African art as primitive, and by primitive meant that it was the product of people incapable of understanding their feelings—love or hate, spiritual wonder or cosmic anguish, were all unpremeditated expressions. The idea that African artists worked without rules and stylistic precedents was the same sort of mistake that Europeans and Americans had earlier made about African societies, when they concluded that the societies contained no rules for personal or community behavior

ANIMAL FERTILITY SYMBOLS *decorate this wooden door guarding the shrine of a Senufo secret society. The life-giving spirits of the turtle, crocodile, antelope and hornbill are represented by the stylized carved figures around the edges; the central panel shows horsemen and crop-bearing fields around a symbolic sun disk. The object at upper left is the door handle and lock.*

because none were visible. Similarly, they were unable to perceive any recognizable sign of discipline in African art, and so assumed it was primitive. This mistake was partly the result of historical accident.

It so happened that the sculpture that arrived in Paris in the early 1900s came largely from peoples upon whom it was easy to tack the label "primitive." The masks included those of the Dan, Senufo, Baule and Kota peoples who lived in the Ivory Coast and the northwest Congo. They were worn, along with raffia robes, in religious dances, and they depicted snarling monsters and other strange creatures of the imagination. To Europeans, accustomed to evaluating feelings according to their degree of refinement, the emotions expressed in these objects must indeed have seemed wildly uncontrolled. Also, many of the stylized figures carved by these peoples were so removed from portraiture or likeness that they must have seemed the work of untutored hands—like the art of children. The fact that experimental artists like Picasso admired and used African art in their fight against representational art also helped to fix the label of "primitive."

But if Picasso and the other radical spokesmen for an abstract art had lived in Berlin instead of Paris, they might well have disregarded African art. For in Berlin there arrived, during the same period, African art of a very different sort. German travelers returning from Nigeria brought with them a number of bronze heads and plaques from Benin. Though often curious in style and ornamentation, this work was clearly not primitive. On the contrary, it depicted figures recognizable as people, and was obviously meant to serve familiar purposes—such as enhancing royal prestige. Unable to connect the Benin sculpture with their notion of a primitive Africa, critics and scholars looked for an exotic origin. One German scholar, Leo Frobenius, suggested that Benin's art might be descended

AFRICA'S IMPACT on Western art is suggested in this comparison of a stone head by the Italian modernist Amedeo Modigliani (above) and a ritual mask carved by a Fang tribesman (right). The Italian artist first saw African carvings in Paris in the early 1900s and was inspired by them

istortions and powerful abstract forms. Though Modiliani's style is clearly original, many of his hallmarks—he elongated face, the small, pursed mouth, the almond-haped eyes and double-lined eyebrows—are clearly deived from similar elements in traditional African art.

from the art of the long-lost continent of Atlantis.

During the 1930s, the idea that African art was the product of simple men and raw emotion became even more difficult to support. Archeologists, digging around the site of the old Yoruba city of Ife in southwest Nigeria, came upon a number of superbly "classical" bronze and terra-cotta heads. For a time these too were generally attributed to some non-African source, or at least to some non-African influence. Since Africans were incapable of human portraiture, it was argued, these splendid heads must be the consequence of some foreign intrusion; perhaps some wandering Renaissance sculptor had found his way to Ife, and there introduced a new art which flourished with him while he lived, and died when he died.

Most of these early explanations of African art have been undermined by more recent research—not only into African art but into the nature of art in general. The majestic heads and figures of Ife and Benin are as much a product of Africa as are the monster-masks of the Senufo and the geometrical abstractions of the Kota. The apparent conflict between them is one of artistic style, not artistic ability. They were all conceived by artists working within an intensely religious culture whose rituals were hallowed by tradition. Consequently, whatever an artist contributed out of his own fund of skill and imagination (and there were of course greater and less talents) had also to fit into an established mold. This was not as arbitrary as it may sound. To the pagan African, art was what missals and prayer books are to the Christian: a guide to religious ritual and religious experience.

Most of the art of Africa has had this consciously religious function. The sculpture, the dances, the drum music and the songs have been designed to reinforce the workings of the force within nature that animates all life—the creative energy from which all blessings flow. It is an art that is nothing

if not dynamic, since it attempts to give material form to an abstraction. And it is quite the reverse of primitive, for instead of being the instinctive expression of one man's immediate feelings, it is the distillation of a long collective process of spiritual experiment. To understand the spiritual content of this art and interpret its symbolism, it is necessary to understand the religion—a task the non-African world has only just begun. Nevertheless, in the last few decades some of the crucial riddles of African art have been solved.

How old is traditional African art? What governed its local variations, and why did these take the forms they did? Under what circumstances did individual talent alter conventional forms? In answering these questions it is easiest to use sculpture for an example, since—unlike music and dancing —it has left records that can be placed side by side with recent developments for study and comparison.

The tradition of sculpture in Africa begins with the Iron Age because no examples exist from before that time—although undoubtedly Stone Age Africans sculpted, since Saharan rock paintings show them to have been skillful artists. In the 1940s, Bernard Fagg, an archeologist working in Nigeria, discovered a collection of terra-cotta heads and pieces of figures in the waste from tin mines.

They showed an astonishing range of stylistic invention and artistic skill. Presently they were collected and housed in a museum at Jos, in central Nigeria, where they were studied more systematically. Archeological tests indicated that they had been deposited over a period of 700 years, beginning around 500 B.C.

From the name of the village where the fragments were found, the peoples who produced them were called the Nok culture. And from the archeological tests and studies there soon emerged two startling implications. One was that the Nok culture probably marked the beginning of the Iron Age in West Africa—since Nok figures are generally found with early iron-working equipment, notably with the clay tubes that were used to connect bellows to primitive blast furnaces. The second was that the Nok peoples appear to have been the cultural ancestors of the Yoruba peoples, who produced the sculpture of Ife many centuries later.

Both the Nok and Ife figures can be almost life-sized, and both use a distinctive proportion: the head is one third to one quarter the size of the body, and thus seems out of scale. Apparently this was done deliberately. Believing the head to be the seat of the life force, the sculptors gave it more importance. Perhaps for the same reason, Nok and Ife sculptors modeled the head more carefully than

NIGERIA'S BRILLIANT HERITAGE *of sculpture is illustrated by these three heads, which span more than 1,700 years. The powerful figure at far left was fashioned in terra cotta by an artist of the Nok culture about 200 B.C. The superbly naturalistic head in the center was cast in brass at Ife in the 13th Century. (The facial lines are probably ancient tribal markings; the holes may be places to attach beaded ornaments.) The bronze at right, its face set off by an intricate headdress and necklaces, represents the highest artistic achievements of 16th Century Benin.*

the body and limbs, which are given scant attention. But if Nok and Ife are related, as these similarities in style indicate, there is a missing link. While Nok culture appears to have come to an end around the year 200, the sculpture of Ife apparently did not begin until around the 13th Century. Perhaps someday archeologists will find the relics of some intervening culture.

In the meantime, while the evidence for a connection between the Nok and Ife cultures is very strong, the two also have their stylistic differences. The faces of Ife heads have Nok features, but they are much more obviously representational. Some of them, in fact, look like individual portraits. If they were, it is not difficult to guess what prompted them. The peoples of 13th Century Ife had developed a far more complex way of life than the peoples of Iron Age Nok. They had city-states with kings and ruling families, courts and court ceremonials. Like other potentates, these rulers used art to describe and celebrate their temporal and spiritual importance; Ife art was court art.

But it was not only that. In an Ife tomb excavated at Abiri in 1949, archeologists found a variety of terra-cotta figures, some of them realistic and some of them decidedly not. Three are superb examples of human portraiture; one is a fine ram, another a coiled snake. Along with these, however, was a group of small conical objects with crudely modeled human features. It is unreasonable to assume that some of the artists were capable of producing portraits while others were not. Obviously these were two different kinds of art, serving two different religious purposes. One was probably memorial and the other probably magical, following some ancient religious convention.

After Ife, the tradition of West African sculpture passed to Benin, where once again artists mixed new styles with old. Benin too had a court art. Between 1550 and 1690 its powerful and wealthy kings commissioned sculptors to embellish the great palace. Benin's sculptors made many fine heads and figures for this building, but they are also famous for the bronze plaques which once decorated the courtyard columns—and now decorate many museums. The plaques are a fascinating record of Benin life for a period of about 140 years; they even portray the early Portuguese explorers who visited Benin in the 16th Century.

But the Nok-Ife-Benin progression is only a small part of the African sculptural tradition. Other kinds of sculpture branched off from it or grew up alongside it at unknown points in time. In the 1930s archeologists digging at Esie in western Nigeria came upon a mysterious cache of stone figures in a slightly different style but of undeniably fine workmanship. To this day, no one knows who made them. Similarly, a group of exceptionally beautiful bronze figures found in a region adjacent to Benin, and originally assumed to be the work of Benin sculptors, now turns out to have been done by related peoples living along the lower Niger River. But the identity of these peoples is unknown.

When it comes to wood-carved sculpture, the problem of dating and tracing becomes even more difficult. One reason for this is the sheer abundance of the work. In spite of the ravages of the white ant, which can reduce a small log to powder in a matter of months, there are more surviving examples of African wood sculpture than of either clay or bronze. Africans carved in wood prolifically and with an inspired hand. No other peoples have outshone them, and few have approached their level of technical virtuosity and conceptual daring. Even so, not all Africans carved equally well. Most of the best work seems to come from the regions of the savanna and dense tropical rain forest, and within these regions it is fairly easy to sort out styles. There are the snarling helmet masks of the Senufo, the graceful antelope figures of the Bambara, the flat geometrical shapes of the Kota. But other styles are not so clearly associated with specific peoples, and are even more troublesome to date—especially to date with reference to their position in the long scale of African sculptural development.

Few of the existing wood carvings in Africa are likely to be more than 30 years old because wood has a short life in the tropics. How closely, then, do the existing examples resemble their antecedents? How much have they changed in style with the passage of time? If the changes in metal and terracotta sculpture are any guide, the answer is that they have probably changed substantially in their details but very little in their essential forms. Yet in one way the works in more durable materials offer an unreliable parallel. Since metal and terra-cotta figures lasted through many generations, to be seen and used and to become ever more venerable with age, the artist was much less free to break with artistic convention and use his own imagination. He was likely to produce works closely modeled on those of the past.

Wood carvers, of course, were also expected to follow convention, but in their case the models were short-lived. Mold and the diligent white ant substantially removed any chance for older works to fix their details upon the work of subsequent generations. Consequently, along with the recurring need for new works, there was also a greater opportunity for variation in form; there was far less copying, and much more dependence upon individual skill and imagination. This explains why any large collection of African wood carvings is likely to contain examples of master carvers alongside the work of men with little or no talent at all: a really fine craftsman might raise the level of excellence for his generation, only to see it brought down again by his less-gifted grandson.

To non-Africans, sculpture may well seem the greatest of the African traditional arts—because that is the art they most often see. But to Africans, the most important art is dancing. Dance fuses the two central concerns of African life: religion and community relationships. It is sometimes ceremonial, marking the start of a hunt or the end of a harvest; sometimes ritual, in observance of birth and death, puberty and marriage; sometimes festive, honoring the special days of the gods and spirits who guard the village. Sometimes it is just recreational. Except for esoteric events, dancing generally involves the whole village. Men, women and even little children—bobbing on the fringes of the adult dancers like corks on a swelling tide—move in response to complex and compelling rhythms. The source of the rhythm is almost invariably drums, for drumming is the music of Africa.

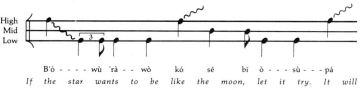

B'ó - - - - wù 'rà - - wò kó sē bĩ ò - - - sù - - - pá
If   the   star   wants   to   be   like   the   moon,   let   it   try.   It   will

Ó - - lò - - rūn Ō - - bã ò fún - - 'rà - - wò sē - - nĩ.
fail,   because   Almighty   God   did   not   endow   it   with   such   powers.

THE TALKING DRUM *of the Yoruba people in Nigeria has strings that, when squeezed, vary the tension on the drumhead so that it can produce notes ranging over an octave or more. By using a curved drumstick, and changing the pitch and rhythm of his sounds, a skillful drummer can "talk" with his drum in a special drum language based on the distinct tonal patterns of the tribe's spoken language. Drum talking is used for sending messages, leading dances or reciting traditional Yoruba proverbs like the one illustrated above.*

The drums of Africa have many different sounds and are played in many different combinations. Some have the familiar drumhead of skin, and can be tuned to various graduations of pitch—high, medium, low. Often, several of these are tuned in a scale, and played together as a drum choir. But not all African drums are this conventional. The tension drum, shaped like an hourglass, is strung with cords that, when pressed, cause subtle changes in pitch. And the slit drum is a hollowed-out log in which a carefully carved opening provides the necessary resonance. In addition, many of the drums are festooned with rattles made of various materials—stones, gourds, shells, cocoons—that add an obbligato of buzzing or rasping sounds to the main beat.

Africans drummed on rocks long before they knew how to stretch hides over hollow logs, and their technical proficiency is spectacular. A good African drummer can literally make his drum speak in words and sentences by varying the strength and placement of his tapping to reproduce the sounds of African speech. The "talking drums" of Africa are not fictions, but a real means of communication. "I was told," wrote the English traveler A. B. Lloyd in 1899, "that from one village to another, a distance of over 100 miles, a message could be sent in less than two hours, and I quite believe it possible for it to be done in much less time."

The most astonishing element in African drumming is not sound, however, but rhythm. Unlike Western music, which is built on simple rhythmic patterns, like the one-two-three, one-two-three of the waltz, African drumming is polyrhythmic. After the opening bars, in which the master drummer announces the theme, each drummer takes up a complementary variation and elaborates upon it, crisscrossing it and weaving it into the rhythms of the other drummers to create a dense tapestry of sound. Most non-Africans cannot follow the intricacies of African drum music much beyond the introductory bars. But Africans hear each rhythm as a distinct pattern, frequently picking out one to follow with their feet, while the other parts of their bodies follow other rhythms—shoulders moving to one, feet to another, heads to still a third.

Sometimes this dancing is spontaneous and everyone participates. But on great occasions it is strictly choreographed and may only be done by trained dancers. Like the masks designed to be worn on these occasions, the dances are associated with certain gods and ancestral spirits, or certain religious rites—of birth, marriage, death—and must follow prescribed forms. Even the drums for such occasions are sacred, and in many societies are housed separately from other drums. Dancers and drummers engage in a ritual dialogue, and both "talk" continuously to the audience. Often the combination of insistent rhythm and dynamic response sends the dancers into a trance. Thus rhythm appeals to more than the senses; it is the route to the power that motivates life, a mystical experience.

There is a similar, although much less intense, dramatic interplay in the African art of storytelling. The storyteller, usually the oldest person in the village, enlivens his tale with all sorts of sound effects. He changes the pitch and pace of his voice to suit the characters and the action, and adds all sorts of popping, clicking, clapping noises to dramatize what is happening. The members of the audience respond in kind, rather like a chorus. They interpose comments at conventional intervals, add their own sound effects, sing any songs that occur in the tale. In short, they are part of the performance. But at the same time they are receiving a message. Like folk tales everywhere, African folk tales are parables and fables that are meant to instruct as well as please. And since Africa's traditional literature is entirely oral, the folk tale is a vital force in community life. It tells people about their his-

tory, teaches them morality, comments on politics, and explains human nature and changing social customs.

Africans especially enjoy folk tales about animals and insects with a reputation for quirky character. One of their favorites is the Great Spider, Ananse Kokrofo, who is sometimes regarded as the symbol of the Supreme Deity. Ananse is wily, witty, full of mischief, and determined to be chief of everything. One day, so the story goes, Ananse decided to collect all the wisdom in the world for himself, and hide it in a gourd. For safety, he proposed to keep the gourd at the top of a tree. So he tied it to his stomach and started to climb. But halfway up he encountered trouble; the gourd hampered his movements. His son, Ntikuma, watching from below, twitted him irreverently: "Father," he called, "if you really had all the wisdom in the world up there with you, you would have put the gourd on your back." At which Ananse, recognizing the truth of Ntikuma's remark, threw down the gourd in a temper. When it struck the ground, it broke, scattering wisdom far and wide, and men ran to gather up whatever they could find. But no man got more than a little bit.

Africa's high arts, like Ananse's gourd full of wisdom, are now largely splintered and scattered. This is not necessarily because other arts have supplanted them, but because Africa has changed. The old Africa, of which these arts were so integral a part, has now lost much of its meaning and coherence. Although traditional art is still practiced seriously by a few good African artists, much of what is called traditional art is nothing but commercial rubbish. Here and there, however, other artists are seeking to bridge the gap between the old and the new—not by re-creating the past, but by recognizing their affinity with the spirit that animated the past, and from that affinity creating a new art for modern Africa.

GLEAMING, DISTORTED, INTENSE, *a Guro female figure embodies the peculiar power of African sculpture.*

VIGOROUS SHAPES IN WOOD

Although styles of sculpture varied widely among African tribes, all shared a common purpose: to express in material form the mystical spirits and "life force" preached by a unique religion. Since the West has no direct experience of such a religious climate, some critics believe that African art is "beyond our horizons." Yet, through the selective eye of photographer Eliot Elisofon, a student and collector of Central and West African sculpture, many of the powerful qualities of this art become clear: the brilliant carving, the three-dimensional depth, the surface textures, and—most important—the emotional impact that comes from translating into solid wood the extraordinary shapes of abstract ideas.

A DOGON ANCESTOR FIGURE, *shown in three views, reflects the powerful spirit it was carved to house. The figure is 16 inches high.*

A STYLIZED DOLL, *with a round head and elongated neck, was tucked in an Ashanti woman's waistband as a plea for a beautiful baby.*

HOUSES FOR SPIRITS

In Africa, tribal sculpture was seldom created to be enjoyed as "art." Rather, each piece was designed to attract and contain specific religious spirits. An ancestor figure such as the one seen at far left was carved as a home for the spirit of a long-dead chieftain—a spirit which otherwise might roam in anger and harm a village. A beautiful doll *(left)* was often fashioned to give sanctuary to the spirit of a child not yet born. Without the presence of such spirits, a piece of sculpture had little value. For example, if a wood carving began to rot or crack and was no longer a suitable home for a spirit, another figure was made to replace it, and the first piece, no matter how beautiful, was discarded as worthless.

AN IRON HORSE AND RIDER, *hammered into slender, balanced curves, added the strength of its spirit to that of the man owning it.*

A RHYTHM POUNDER *(right and above) was held by its arms and thumped on the ground in ritual dances to rouse the earth's life force.*

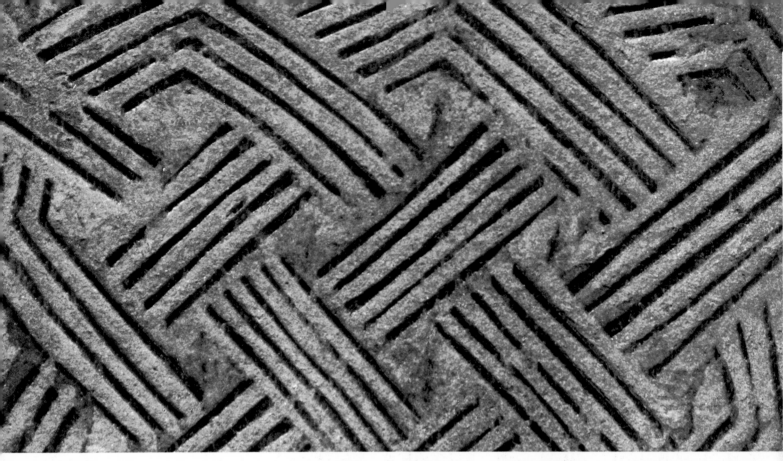

PATTERNS
WITH MEANING

Abstract designs in the form of surface texture and decoration often
had a deep spiritual significance in
African art. Geometric patterns like
the one seen at right (in a detail
from the top of a cosmetic box) were
known to have had mystic powers so
important that they reappeared in
many forms, including ceremonial
scarring and tattooing on certain
tribesmen's bodies and faces. Other
patterns represented the more ordi-
nary spirits that lived in such material objects as fabric and yarn. The
interwoven pattern above, from another box lid, repeats in wood the
design of one of the Bushongo tribe's
distinctive woven cloths; at the far
right, the textured surface on the
arch of a loom's bobbin imitates in
carving the twisted strands of fiber
which rolled over its pulley wheel.

SHAPE AND VARIATION

The eight female heads seen below, arranged by photographer Elisofon in profile and in silhouette, are all decorative tops of pulleys used in weaving by Guro tribesmen. Each follows the Guro artists' traditional style of carving a woman's head with a pronounced forehead curve, pursed lips and roundness at the back. Yet, within this prescribed tradition, individual

artists have stamped their particular work with lively originality—an exaggerated hair arrangement, an ornate neck decoration, a sharp nose. Such variations on an established theme constantly infused new vitality into traditional African carving. If a slightly raised chin or a new inclination of the headdress seemed to give more energy to the figure, this subtle angle was incorporated into the tradition of the tribe's art. The man who could produce added power through sculpture was a valuable member of his society. His kinsmen believed such accomplishments raised him above other men. Praise for the early work of one sculptor was dismissed by a fellow tribesman because it was done "before he became perfect."

FORM AND TENSION

Almost all African sculpture was made from a single piece of wood, selected from a still-growing tree by the sculptor, who scrupulously stayed within the tree's form when he carved. This close collaboration of artist with his material is reflected in the funerary figure seen in three views at right, and in the detail of a man's head above. The figure reflects the single cylinder of wood from which it was made: the arms are held close to the body, the feet are flat to the ground and the head is erect —all lending the body great tension and strength. The head shown above, also taut and erect, illustrates the dramatic detail possible within such a compressed form.

MASKS: MYSTERY IN MOTION

Although much African sculpture was immobile and conveyed its interior energy by a sense of arrested movement, masks were meant to be seen in action. Most wildly imaginative of all African sculpture, their mysterious, tortured and often terrifying lines expressed the ultimate in supernatural forces. Such animalistic masks as the Baule bull's head *(top center)*, the grooved Basonge lion's head *(center)* and the Ngere warthog *(lower right)* were worn during rites of initiation into adult status, as well as in ceremonies of the secret societies in West and Central Africa. These societies varied in nature from mutual assistance groups to sinister cabals, and their funerals, festivals and other important occasions were almost always accompanied by fierce dancing in masks. The harrowing quality of much of this dancing came from the wearer's belief in the spirits represented by the masks—strange forces that were supposed to flood through him. Masked dancers, feeling themselves possessed by these forces, often went into deep trances and danced for hours without stopping.

HIGH ARTISTRY
IN EVERYDAY OBJECTS

The artist's main function within his tribe was to create sculpture for religious purposes, but artistic skill invariably came into play in the making of objects for everyday use. Although such objects frequently were made attractive to please the spirits inhabiting them, sculptors also lavished care on household items out of a traditional pride in their craft. The beauty of these artifacts comes from their blend of function and form. For example, the curved blades and decorated, tapering shaft of the large throwing knife shown here are not only ornamental but give the knife perfect balance. In the cup below, the beautifully carved hands and arms that spring from the base are molded for the easy clasp of fingers, whether the cup is lifted with one hand or two.

A CHIEF'S STOOL *with elongated male and female figures was cut from a solid tree trunk.*

A PALM-WINE CUP *is carved as a man's head supported by arms emerging from its base.*

A THROWING KNIFE *with a textured ha* *and multiple blades was used to hunt ga*

A LONG-HANDLED SPOON *is subtly balanced by the carved headdress atop its female head.*

ORNATE HEADRESTS *curve to pillow women's necks without disturbing their hairdos.*

A MANY-FACED ANCESTOR
OF MODERN ART

By rotating the five-inch Dogon ancestor figure seen at far left through 180° in multiple exposures *(below)*, photographer Elisofon followed the techniques of cubism to dramatize Africa's contributions to modern art. The photograph clearly shows the African idea of abstraction and emphasis of body parts; the feeling of the original wood block in the firm stance and muscular tension; the surfaces broken into distinct planes; the patina of these planes, preserved and rubbed to a deep glow.

It was precisely these qualities that so impressed the revolutionaries of Western art—Picasso, Braque, Matisse, Derain—when they first encountered them in the early 1900s. Such techniques, which they themselves had been searching for in their efforts to go beyond strict representation of natural forms, gradually appeared in radically new movements such as cubism and surrealism. Today, below surface changes, these same African traditions still flow deep in the mainstream of modern Western art.

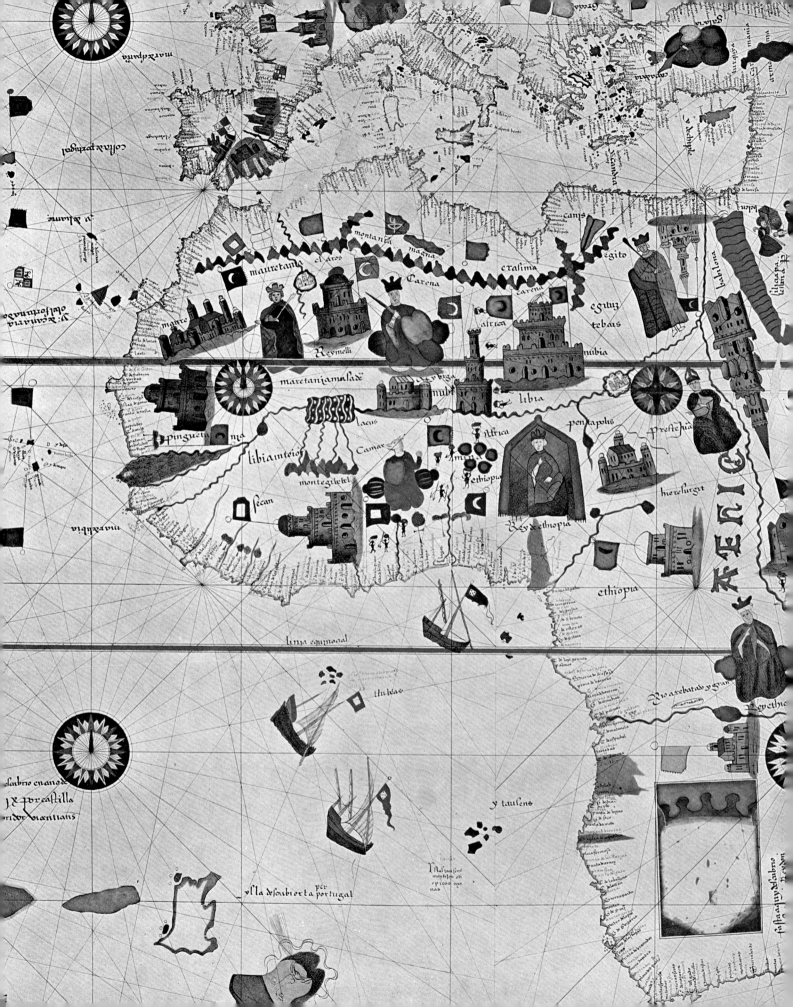

8

A CONTINENT TRIUMPHANT

Although many of tropical Africa's most impressive achievements occurred from the 10th to the 16th Centuries, to most Westerners the continent's history did not really begin until the European powers took over. In the 19th Century, when the nations of Europe had finally settled among themselves which was to have what in the Americas and the East, they turned their attention to Africa in their search for new markets and colonial sites. By the end of the century they had remade the whole African map, drawing the boundaries according to their own relative military strength or aggressiveness at the conference table, and often without regard to the existing social and political structures in Africa.

The invaders, cutting their confident way through hostile forests and out across grasslands tawny as a lion's mane, and finding what seemed to them a wild human confusion, made a great and sudden silence around themselves and called it peace. "The guns and Maxims [machine guns] having been brought into action," ran a typical contemporary report, "the [British-led troops] reached the river bank without halting, and the Fulah force broke up and retired within the city. Nothing now remained but to shell the place."

As a matter of fact a great deal of the same sort of persuasion remained, even if much of it was carried out with the best of intentions. The invaders were determined that civilized institutions were to shed their peaceful light—by force, if necessary—over peoples who were thought to possess no institutions of their own.

Yet even then, in that heyday of brash imperialism, there were misgivings. At least a few critical observers questioned whether the new trustees had any real notion of what they were so wantonly destroying. Perhaps no one put this view more pointedly—or wittily—than the intelligent young Victorian traveler Mary Kingsley, whose writings were all the harder to set aside because she had had much experience in Africa. Miss Kingsley repeatedly chided the colonial powers for abolishing political systems that they did not understand, and for then showing pained surprise when the natives failed to reveal a proper gratitude.

The imperial story, she wrote, was very like

A EUROPEAN VIEW *of Africa is reflected in this Spanish map of 1500. Even the dry Sahara is crowded with European-looking kings, prelates and castles—many of them ranged along a forked Nile that runs west to the coast.*

"that improving fable of the kind-hearted she-elephant who, while out walking one day, inadvertently trod upon a partridge and killed it, and observing close at hand the bird's nest full of callow fledglings, dropped a tear, and saying 'I have the feelings of a mother myself,' sat down upon the brood. This is precisely what England representing the 19th Century is doing in . . . West Africa. She destroys the guardian institution, drops a tear and sits upon the brood with motherly intentions; and," added Miss Kingsley as the sound of distant gunfire echoed from beyond the forest skyline, "pesky warm sitting she finds it."

Pesky warm it certainly proved. Because of the strength of Africa's "guardian institutions," wars of pacification were to continue in many regions until the 1920s. The critics, ignored at the time, were afterward remembered when the validity and power of precolonial institutions that had offered long resistance to conquest became a favored theme among those who spoke for the African side of the question.

"To put it shortly," said a veteran African protagonist of early nationalism, the Gold Coast's Joseph Ephraim Caseley Hayford, in a 1920 address to a London audience, "before ever the British came into relations with our people, we were a developed people, having our own institutions, having our own ideas of government." Much later, while the slogans of a renewed independence drummed in the African air, another generation would say the same. "Men on other parts of this earth occupied themselves with their own concerns," declared the Emperor of Ethiopia when opening a conference on African unity in 1963, "and, in their conceit, proclaimed that the world began and ended at their horizons. All unknown to them, Africa developed in its own pattern, growing in its own life."

These statements argued a political case, but they also spoke for a deeper reality. The nature of this precolonial reality can be examined, now that the colonial period is largely past, in less emotional language. It becomes possible to answer several large questions about the African past in ways that can at last give Africans their due place in the story of mankind.

Against a background of world history, what was the human value of traditional African civilization, of its teachings, its beliefs, and its political and moral patterns of behavior? Where and how have Africans contributed to the sum of man's achievement? Will some aspects of that old culture still play a part in shaping the developing Africa today? Over the past two decades of historical reconstruction, students of Africa have returned a number of replies of varying worth.

Significantly, much of the answer can be best discovered by observing the African influence on the Western Hemisphere. The history of the Americas would have been a very different one without the great contribution made by African labor, African arts and African skills. The African's role in the growth of the sugar and tobacco plantations of the Caribbean and North America is well known. Less familiar is the African contribution in other fields. At least until the early 19th Century, the mines of Brazil were mainly worked by Africans who had learned their skill at home.

The Negroes also lent something of the traditional African style to the American crafts in which they engaged, and they engaged in many. "I have now," an American traveler could say of Brazil in the mid-19th Century, "seen slaves working as carpenters, masons, pavers, printers, sign and ornamental painters, carriage and cabinet makers, fabricators of military ornaments, lamp-makers, silversmiths, jewellers, and lithographers." If the slaves made many things that Africa had never known, they nevertheless created them with the artistry and skill that derived from their native culture.

Why then should Africans at home have failed to develop their own industries? The answer lies in a consideration of those qualities and limitations of traditional African culture that combined an outstanding aptitude for the arts with a backwardness in the sciences—a characteristic typical of all pretechnological societies. The consequent attitudes resulted in approaches to everyday problems that were often highly experimental—and, at the same time, imbued with a profound conservatism that was itself a product of long stability and ingrained tradition.

Facing the supremacy of an industrialized Europe in the 19th Century, meeting machine guns with spears, or bows and arrows, or ancient firearms of imported manufacture, the Africans were in a large sense victims of their own past adaptability to their native environment. Most of the continent's populations, cut off from the outside world by seas of sand and water, had worked out preindustrial ways of living that were adequate to survival and even to a fair degree of comfort. Real information is scant, but the available evidence suggests that most peoples south of the Sahara had a standard of living far above the minimum subsistence level, and enjoyed a reasonably secure life. Having this, and lacking industrial examples, they had little motivation to strive for more.

But the key condition was always present: to achieve a comfortable existence, or even bare survival, traditional practices had to be observed. Hence the Africans' often fanatical distrust of change. So long as the Dinka, for example, were careful to follow the annual regulation of their cattle camps and sowing seasons, they would be sure of a year's supplies. Let them seriously depart from these well-tried practices, and disaster might ensue. Haphazard though their community organization might seem to the uninstructed eye, it was really shaped and fashioned in every detail to a framework of harsh ecological necessity.

In every detail: here, of course, lies the central point about Africa's guardian institutions. For the Dinka met their needs—and were bound to do so if they were going to survive—by observing not only strict farming rules, but also a network of religious, social and political beliefs and customs that ensured that the rules would be kept. This network had to be flexible enough to allow a tolerance for individual error, for occasional disputes between different groups of kin, and for periods of natural adversity; but more than that, it had to be strong enough to absorb such troubles, and to insist, sternly and inexorably, on the continued stability of Dinka society. During centuries of trial and error, as peoples such as these spread across their continent and learned to survive on it, systems emerged that were carefully balanced against the various threats to life.

By about 1800 A.D., the centuries of such experiment in traditional Africa—Iron-Age Africa—were practically over. Most of its systems had developed to their point of ultimate maturity. Rural prosperity, based firmly on methods of production for more or less immediate consumption or exchange, depended not on expanding the overall supply of goods but on steadily maintaining it. Most Africans were farmers or craftsmen, and the farmer or craftsman usually felt he needed not a bigger market but a continued assurance of the market he already had. His ideal was to live in the manner of his forebears; so long as this was possible, all would be well.

"Good behavior, respect for elders, and conformity to the life led by one's fathers, seeking little or no wealth or position": these admonitions of the guardian spirits of the Shona people of Rhodesia were not exceptional. Abnormalities of ambition or behavior were to be condemned: what was good was what was usual, and what was usual was laid down by the teachings of ancestors. Having tamed their continent and made it serve them, African communities did not welcome the idea of progress, because progress would mean change, and change could only threaten the subtle balance that man and nature had wrought between them.

The beginning of the 19th Century marks a clear dividing line, because it was followed by a very different situation. At that point, the factors making for disintegration began to overwhelm the old stability and peace. One of these new elements was the tremendous eruption of Nguni peoples out of southeastern Africa into the central plateau and as far north as the great lakes of the east. Another was the growth of a new and destructive slave trade inland through East Africa from the Arab-ruled island of Zanzibar. A third was the Muslim religious war which unsettled many of the formerly stable regimes of West Africa. Finally there was the mounting pressure and penetration of Europeans. Large regions were increasingly engulfed in tumult and upheaval.

Yet the great achievement of stability and peace stands clearly in the record until about 1800. Even today, in the oral history of many peoples, one may catch the glimmer of its long nostalgic afterglow, dignified and serene. One or two descriptions of that evening of traditional maturity were also written at the time by Africans themselves. In Europe's great year of revolution, 1789, a former slave from Iboland in eastern Nigeria, Olaudah Equiano, published a book about his homeland. Though somewhat idealized for the purposes of the anti-slavery campaign, this Nigerian account strikes an authentic note.

"As we live in a country where nature is prodigal of her favours, our wants are few, and easily supplied . . . We have plenty of Indian corn, and vast quantities of cotton and tobacco. Our pine ap-

ples grow without culture: they are about the size of the largest sugar-loaf and finely flavoured. We have also spices of different kinds, particularly pepper; and a variety of delicious fruits which I have never seen in Europe. . . . All our industry is exerted to improve those blessings of nature. Agriculture is our chief employment, and every one, even the children and women, are engaged in it. Thus we are all habituated to labour from our earliest years. Every one contributes something to the common stock; and, as we are unacquainted with idleness, we have no beggars."

They also had few manufactured products, Equiano admitted, except cotton cloth, pottery, "ornaments and instruments of war and husbandry." But why should they need more? "In such a state money is of little use . . . In our buildings we study convenience rather than ornament. Each master of a family has a large square piece of ground, surrounded with a moat or fence . . . In the middle stands the principal building, appropriated to the sole use of the master, and consisting of two apartments; in one of which he sits in the day with his family, the other is left apart for the reception of his friends . . . And as our manners are simple, our luxuries are few."

Other accounts confirm the essential accuracy of Equiano's picture. None is more convincing, perhaps, than a down-to-earth report made in 1811 by a pair of traders, the Afro-Portuguese mulattoes Pedro João Baptista and Amaro José. Theirs was a remarkable feat. Nearly half a century before Livingstone and other European pioneers made the crossing of middle Africa, these two traders traversed the greater part of it from west to east, and then quietly back again from east to west, a total of about 4,000 miles. The trip, which they made simply in the way of business, took nine years. Baptista was literate, and wrote a journal of their travels. Two points of great interest emerge from it.

A DUTCH DELEGATION, *shown prostrate before the King of Kongo in 1642, came to make an alliance, but Portuguese and Spaniards had arrived there first. The King, wearing European boots and a miniature gold cross on one elbow, sits beneath an imported chandelier; the inscription above his throne hails him as "Don Alvare."*

The first is that the peoples whom they passed on their way through middle Africa, like those of Iboland in western Africa described by Equiano a little earlier, had attained by 1800 an easy and even comfortable mode of everyday life. "The territory of Kazembe," wrote Baptista of what is now part of Katanga in the southeastern Congo, "is supplied with provisions all the year round and every year: manioc flour, millet, maize, large haricot beans . . . fruits . . . as bananas, sugar-canes, yams . . . and much fish." There was also a variety of livestock, he reported, including oxen and goats.

But the second point, concerning law and order in territories afterward notorious for their lack of either, is even more interesting. Baptista and Amaro told their Portuguese employers that clear across this vast stretch of Africa, between inland Angola on the west and inland Mozambique on the east, the way was easy enough to follow, provided only that the goodwill of two powerful authorities was assured. These were the rulers of two great states that dominated the whole region, the one being centered on the upper waters of the Kasai River and the other on the Luapula River. Once these monarchs, the Mwata Yamvo and the Mwata Kazembe, or their counselors, were satisfied by appropriate gifts and proof of peaceable intentions, the law was on the side of travelers, and the law would prevail. Much of the precolonial Congo, in other words, offered an orderly and peaceful contrast to the violence and confusion of later times.

Some of the first European pioneers of the inland country were early enough to catch a glimpse of the old way of life before the upheavals of the 19th Century began sweeping it away. In 1831 two Portuguese explorers, Major José Maria Monteiro and Captain Antonio Candido Gamitto, made their way from Mozambique to the court of the reigning Mwata Kazembe. There they confirmed the observations of the two mulatto traders of 20 years earlier. The Kazembe's was a powerful state, but it was also a comfortable one. "We certainly never expected to find," Gamitto wrote afterward, "so much ceremonial, pomp and ostentation in the potentate of a region so remote from the seacoast, and in a nation which appears so barbarous and savage."

Some 40 years later another adventurer, Henry Morton Stanley, returned a comparable judgment on the Ugandan kingdom of the Ganda and its King Mutesa. Visiting this court in 1875, he remarked in his notebook that Mutesa was neither the "tyrannous savage" nor "wholesale murderer" of current European fable, "but a pious Mussulman and an intelligent humane king reigning absolutely over a vast section of Africa, loved more than hated, respected more than feared." Better acquaintance with Ganda history has shown since then that Stanley was exaggerating somewhat; yet he was certainly right in the substance of what he wrote. Mutesa's kingdom of the Ganda possessed a well-functioning system of law and order. Long past the experimental stage, it was, in Stanley's time, already more than three centuries old, Mutesa being about 18th in the line of Ganda kings who had first assumed the throne about 1600 A.D. And what was true of the country of Mutesa or the Kazembe was also true of the greater part of Africa south of the Sahara. Nearly everywhere, in ways that differed greatly in detail, a political stability had come about as the result of all those past experiments in social relations and productive techniques.

This stability was not, of course, either universal or permanent. States that had kings suffered from dynastic conflicts. In western Africa the coastal demand for captives who could be sold as slaves encouraged a host of damaging border raids. Elsewhere there was no lack of petty fights and clashes. But these, as often as not, amounted to little more than a brandishing of spears and a taking of prisoners who could be ransomed for cattle and other goods. In comparison with what came afterward, Africa was at peace.

A catalogue of the African states then existing would be long and complex. In 1800 the Monomotapa empire, which held sway over much of modern Rhodesia, was well into its fourth century. Northward the greater part of the Congo basin, along with its periphery, was enclosed in a series of states of various sizes. Westward the old empire of Oyo in Nigeria still existed, while that of Benin had not yet lost its dignity or power, and Ashanti had still to reach its zenith. If the great empires of the medieval Western Sudan were now no more than a memory, glittering dimly with a vanished glory, others had taken their place. And among them lay a number of lesser systems, some with kings or central authorities and others without, most of which could also claim, like the Dinka and Tallensi, Nyakyusa and Tonga, to have solved the major problems of life at a preindustrial level and to have reached, within those limits, a true stability.

But African conservatism was far from universal or complete. It often proved highly adaptable, particularly wherever the pressures of trade had become important. Arriving in the northern Nigerian town of Kano in the middle of the 19th Century, the German traveler Heinrich Barth, in some ways the most perceptive of all the 19th Century explorers, found that the products of the Kano cotton-weaving industry were being sold all the way from the shores of the Atlantic to the fringes of the forests of the Congo.

This Kano industry, Barth calculated, might annually be worth as much as three hundred million *kurdi* (a currency unit reckoned generally in cowrie shells), "and how great this national wealth is will be understood by my readers," Barth went on to explain, "when they know that, with from fifty to sixty thousand *kurdí,* or from four to five pounds sterling a year, a whole family may live in that country with ease, including every expense, even that of their clothing."

Yet the picture should be completed with a reminder that this was strictly a handicraft industry, and that even its relatively advanced methods of exchange and transport continued to be restricted by traditional rules and customs. If the structure of society underwent many reforms, it never underwent any radical changes. When the machine guns arrived upon the scene, half a century after Barth, they could not be met with effective retaliation. (Whence the bitter words of one of England's anti-imperialist poets, Hilaire Belloc, when he mocked invaders who could boast: "It little matters what they do, for we have got the Maxim gun, and they have not.")

This relative isolation from the outside world was intensified by the action of a string of trading states along the seaboard. Their interest was to erect and maintain a middleman monopoly between the maritime Europeans and the producer peoples of the inland regions. At least until the 1850s, they were generally successful in this attempt. By interposing themselves between the Europeans and inland Africa they may have delayed foreign invasion, but they also prevented the inland peoples from having any opportunity to prepare for the challenge of Europe.

The adaptability of African conservatism was often more marked among these coastal states than elsewhere. While remaining within the framework of a civilization that produced for immediate use or trade rather than for saving and investment, some of these states displayed a viable capacity to adjust themselves to new opportunities. They married the customs of tradition to new methods of trade, some of which were actually early forms of capitalism. Their "corporations," based on trading canoes that could carry scores of men, could enable an intelligent and enterprising man to become a relative tycoon.

The Nigerian town of Brohimi startlingly revealed at the end of the 19th Century how much could be done—but also what could not be done—by these partial changes and reforms. Here the pressures of a different world had long made themselves felt through the slave trade and the presence of the British on the island of Lagos, 150 miles away. What effect these pressures could have was shown, in a curious combination of new ideas with old, by the work of Brohimi's energetic Chief Nana.

Opposing British penetration, Nana repulsed a British "punitive force" in 1894. Here we see one kind of adaptability: Nana had taken good care to learn from British partners before they turned into enemies. Struggling through Brohimi's surrounding swamps and creeks, the invading force found Nana's township girdled by gun positions, the first of which was equipped with 23 cannon "loaded, trained, and primed" (though the gunners failed to fire them) and with charges consisting of "three-pound balls and tubular bamboo frames filled with broken iron pots."

Going on to attack Brohimi itself, the British came under a warm fire from "at least thirty or forty cannon—in addition to plenty of rifles," some of the cannon being "trained directly down the creek so as to render the approach by boats most hazardous, if not impossible." This proved too much for the punitive force, and a bigger one had to be sent in. Its commanding admiral, having then captured Brohimi, was able to confirm what the earlier expedition had reported. The township's defenses showed months and perhaps years of preparation, "and a considerable amount of intelligence. The guns were admirably placed to meet any attack from the direction expected . . . and were well and strongly mounted," numbering altogether no fewer than 106 of various sizes.

But the admiral also reported something else, and it is this that puts Chief Nana's situation in its true perspective. At Brohimi the British found 8,300 cases of imported European gin, 99,600 bottles in all. Now at first glance this might suggest a gargantuan appetite for alcohol, yet the appearance is misleading. Chief Nana had not collected all this strong drink in anticipation of festive orgies, but because European gin had become an outstanding growth investment. For several years the average price of bottled gin had never ceased to rise on the local barter market, and Chief Nana, in saving nearly a hundred thousand bottles, had shown the foresight of a good investor. But this again is the conservative in action. Chief Nana's savings, however well considered for that time and place, were a capital investment of a narrowly limited king. He was really no more economically advanced than the peasant who turns his profits into gold coins to cache in a sock.

Change, then, continued to make its mark on many traditional societies up to the eve of the colonial period, but it was mainly peripheral change, change at the edges of the continent or in the fringe activities of daily life. Even the subjects of the bustling Chief Nana remained untouched by his frugal propensities: they still stood outside an economy of cash, of money wages and profits, and they lived very much as they had in the years before. Reforms were slow to have any general effect, even along the coast.

With the findings of scientific research and the wisdom of hindsight, the modern world can now draw some general conclusions about traditional Africa. The central value of this series of ancient civilizations was that they enabled men to populate the whole of habitable Africa and to multiply and flourish there and, while carrying this out, to weave a rich fabric of traditional patterns, practices and virtues. All this formed a matrix of behavior and belief that had parallels elsewhere, but was nonetheless uniquely African.

In the course of their long cultural development the Africans made several large, productive contributions to the wealth and progress of the rest of the world. Yet their principal gift to the general heritage of man may probably be found to lie in aspects of life less easily defined than the uses of gold and iron, ivory and skilled labor. Few others dealt in the raw material of human nature with more subtlety or ease, or so successfully welded the interests of the community and the individual. The Africans practiced the art of social happiness, and they practiced it brilliantly.

Out of this there came a number of attitudes, characteristics, and talents that the rest of the world has come to recognize as uniquely African. An enduring gaiety of temperament (so often noted that it has become a cliché, but a true characteristic nonetheless), a certain indomitable optimism and tolerance, a joy in esthetic forms, colors, and sounds, and a genius for producing these.

These attitudes and characteristics have probably had more impact on the Western world than those of any other non-Western culture. They have influenced its painting and sculpture (as in the case of Picasso and his followers), its music (by way of American Negro jazz, blues and spirituals), and its way of looking at life (this also chiefly by way of the Negro American's intimate contact with white Americans).

These are the human values that seem most likely to survive from the African past. They appear destined to endure through the difficult years that lie ahead—to impose their stamp more strongly not only on the rest of the world, but also on the new Africa that is arising in our time where once existed the thriving kingdoms of another century.

TRADITIONAL DESIGNS, *structures like the pole-and-thatch roof of this hut in Cameroon are still being built today exactly as they were centuries ago.*

THE ENDURING FORMS

All over Africa men have left a record of achievement not in documents, but in buildings large and small. The first and most formidable problem of the continent's inhabitants was to find ways to live in an immense and varied landscape of deserts, rain forests, savannas and mountains. Their success in meeting this challenge is still celebrated whenever a village family builds a home *(above)*.

But such simple tribal dwellings were not the only structures raised by Africa's people. Scattered across the continent today are ruins that testify to the greatness and diversity of more advanced civilizations that grew in African soil. Some of these ruins are the relics of kingdoms with firm roots in traditional tribal societies. Others, showing a distinct Muslim influence, suggest the vital role that foreign cultures played. Still others, like the crumbling Portuguese fortress at Kilwa, symbolize a later, darker era in Africa's long and complex past.

CIRCULAR HUTS AND COMPOUNDS *of woven rushes, thatch and mud shelter millet farmers in Chad. Though the village is divided into 600 homes, children a*

ANCIENT VILLAGE PATTERNS

In many parts of the continent today, close-knit villages preserve a living record of Africa's earliest forms of community life. Sometimes simple, sometimes intricate in appearance, these villages show how various ancient peoples learned to temper their particular climate by ingenious uses of the most humble materials—sun-dried mud, grass, wicker, bamboo, woven bark. The folkways of these villages also echo patterns of life evolved long ago for the common good. In many villages, tribesmen still live as part of immense "families" that collectively own land, tend crops and livestock, administer justice—and venerate the ancestors who devised these patterns for them centuries ago.

THICK MUD WALLS, *decorated with Arabic designs, keep Nigerians cool in blazing summer heat.*

sed by the community as a whole. SLENDER STILTS *raise a Dinka dwelling and its storage hut above the flood waters of the Upper Nile.*

ZIMBABWE'S GREAT TEMPLE, *enclosed by a massive wall 800 feet in circumference, housed a tribal king, his wives, courtiers and servants.*

A MONUMENT TO A VANISHED NATION

In 1871 the German geologist Karl Mauch, wandering through Rhodesia, came upon a valley filled with "houses of stone"—Zimbabwe, a massive complex of brush-choked temples and fortifications that he decided must be copies of Solomon's Temple and the Queen of Sheba's palace. But archeologists who later explored the ruins discovered the relics of a vanished African civilization which had erected sweeping granite walls in the pattern of Africa's own circular mud-and-thatch villages.

Zimbabwe's ruins shed new light on a majestic episode in Africa's past. Once a center for a large confederacy of tribes that extended some 500 miles from the Zambezi River to the Transvaal, Zimbabwe reached the height of its prosperity between the 15th and 18th Centuries. Its rulers, a dynasty of kings enriched by gold and ivory tribute, displayed their power by erecting the Great Temple (*above*). This grandiose stone version of a tribal chief's enclosure was the site of ceremonial rites kept well hidden from the public view by an elliptical wall that contained 15,000 tons of cut stone.

GRANITE BLOCKS, *skillfully fitted together without mortar into curving walls that rose as high as 32 feet, line a concealed corridor that leads to an inner ceremonial shrine in the Great Temple.*

A RUINED GATEWAY TO THE WORLD

As Portugal's explorers sailed up Africa's east coast on their way to India, they were filled with awe by such glittering ports as Kilwa, Mombasa, Sofala, Malindi and Zanzibar. These trading centers linked inland kingdoms like Zimbabwe with the East, and their culture drew upon both African and Muslim traditions. In Kilwa's Great Mosque *(below)*, colonists and merchants from Arabia and India worshiped alongside Swahili-speaking Africans whose faces were decorated with strange ceremonial markings. Many of the city's newly rich businessmen, though African born, enhanced their prestige by claiming ancestry among aristocratic families in Persia and Arabia.

Today the ancient stone and coral buildings of these once-thriving cities lie in ruins. In the 16th Century the Portuguese, eager to seize the rich Indian Ocean trade, ravaged the ports, eventually turning the east coast into a commercial backwater whose most valued exports were human slaves.

KILWA'S GREAT MOSQUE *stands in ruins amid the coconut groves that now cover the center of the old city. Built by 12th and 15th Century sultans, the mosque served the Muslim oligarchy that controlled Kilwa's commerce.*

BROKEN VAULTS *of the Great Mosque's main hall rest on columns of coral and concrete. The arches once supported a domed ceiling so impressive that one writer even claimed it rivaled Spain's famous Córdoba Mosque.*

A RELIC OF CONQUEST, *the shell of Kilwa's Gereza fortress commemorates the waves of invaders who arrived on Africa's shores—and who were in turn swe*

way by history's changing tides. Erected by the Portuguese in 1505, and later rebuilt by Arabs, it stands today as empty as the town it was meant to guard.

A Chronological Chart of African Civilizations

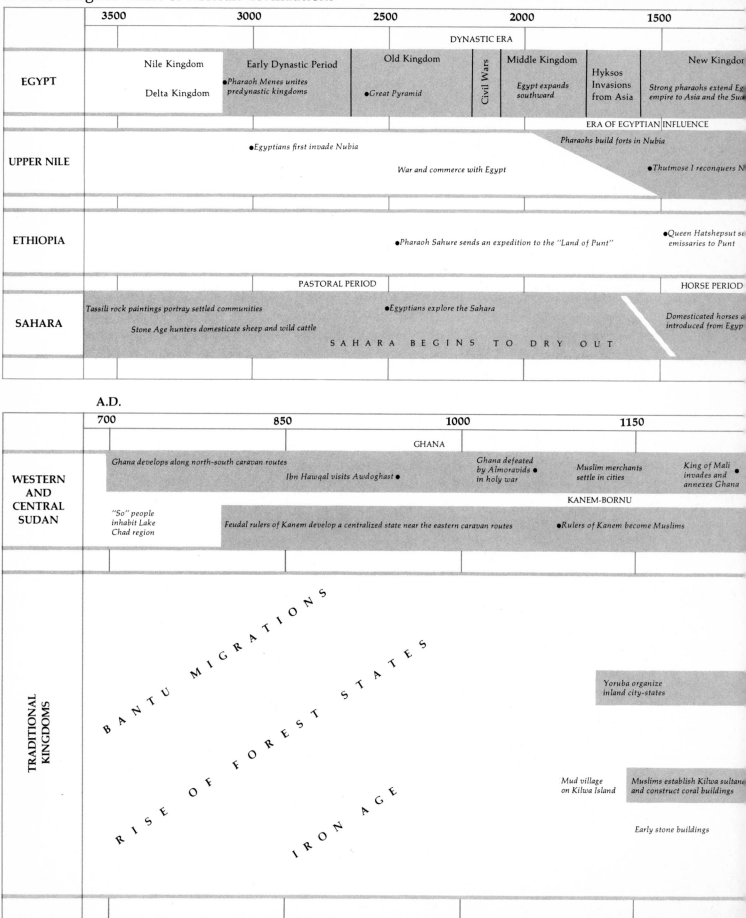

	3500	3000	2500	2000	1500

DYNASTIC ERA

EGYPT

Nile Kingdom · Early Dynastic Period · Old Kingdom · Civil Wars · Middle Kingdom · Hyksos Invasions from Asia · New Kingdom

Delta Kingdom

●Pharaoh Menes unites predynastic kingdoms

●Great Pyramid

Egypt expands southward

Strong pharaohs extend Eg[ypt's] empire to Asia and the Sud[an]

ERA OF EGYPTIAN INFLUENCE

UPPER NILE

●Egyptians first invade Nubia

Pharaohs build forts in Nubia

War and commerce with Egypt

●Thutmose I reconquers N[ubia]

ETHIOPIA

●Pharaoh Sahure sends an expedition to the "Land of Punt"

●Queen Hatshepsut se[nds] emissaries to Punt

PASTORAL PERIOD

HORSE PERIOD

SAHARA

Tassili rock paintings portray settled communities

●Egyptians explore the Sahara

Stone Age hunters domesticate sheep and wild cattle

SAHARA BEGINS TO DRY OUT

Domesticated horses a[re] introduced from Egy[pt]

A.D.

	700	850	1000	1150

GHANA

WESTERN AND CENTRAL SUDAN

Ghana develops along north-south caravan routes

Ibn Hawqal visits Awdoghast ●

Ghana defeated by Almoravids ● in holy war

Muslim merchants settle in cities

King of Mali invades and annexes Ghana

KANEM-BORNU

"So" people inhabit Lake Chad region

Feudal rulers of Kanem develop a centralized state near the eastern caravan routes

●Rulers of Kanem become Muslims

TRADITIONAL KINGDOMS

BANTU MIGRATIONS

RISE OF FOREST STATES

IRON AGE

Yoruba organize inland city-states

Mud village on Kilwa Island

Muslims establish Kilwa sultan[ate] and construct coral buildings

Early stone buildings

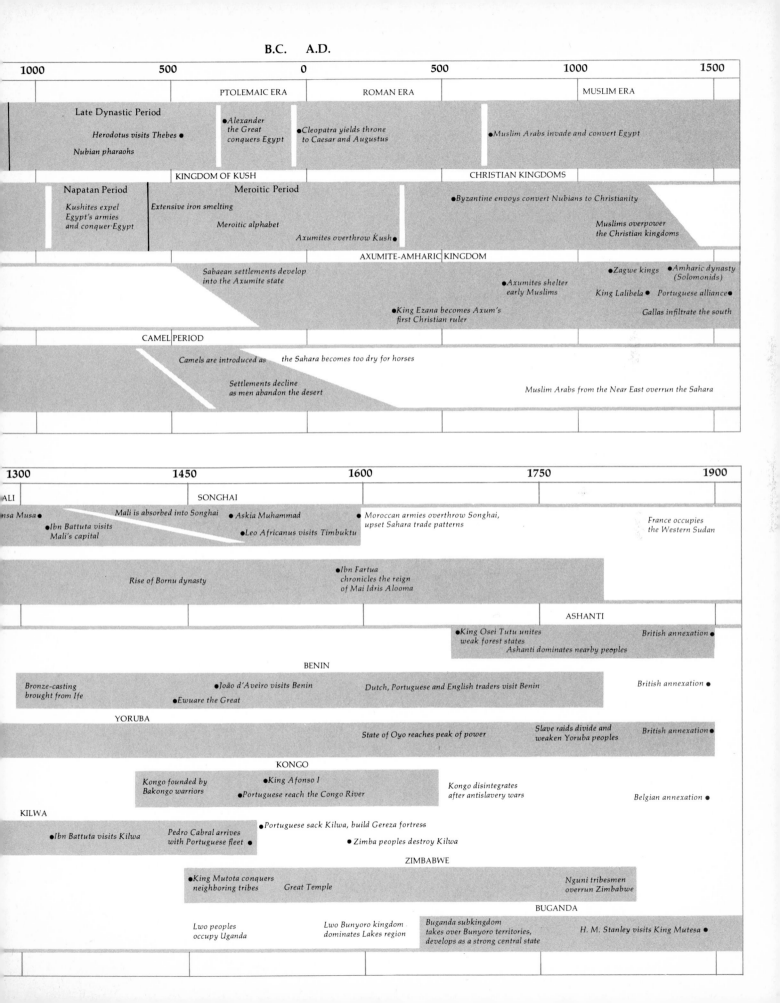

B.C.   A.D.

1000	500	0	500	1000	1500

PTOLEMAIC ERA   ROMAN ERA   MUSLIM ERA

Late Dynastic Period

Herodotus visits Thebes ●

Nubian pharaohs

● *Alexander the Great conquers Egypt*

● *Cleopatra yields throne to Caesar and Augustus*

● *Muslim Arabs invade and convert Egypt*

KINGDOM OF KUSH   CHRISTIAN KINGDOMS

Napatan Period   **Meroitic Period**

Kushites expel Egypt's armies and conquer Egypt

Extensive iron smelting

Meroitic alphabet

Axumites overthrow Kush ●

● *Byzantine envoys convert Nubians to Christianity*

Muslims overpower the Christian kingdoms

AXUMITE-AMHARIC KINGDOM

Sabaean settlements develop into the Axumite state

● *King Ezana becomes Axum's first Christian ruler*

● *Axumites shelter early Muslims*

● *Zagwe kings*

King Lalibela ●

● *Amharic dynasty (Solomonids)*

● *Portuguese alliance* ●

Gallas infiltrate the south

CAMEL PERIOD

Camels are introduced as   *the Sahara becomes too dry for horses*

Settlements decline as men abandon the desert

Muslim Arabs from the Near East overrun the Sahara

1300	1450	1600	1750	1900

ALI   SONGHAI

nsa Musa ●

Mali is absorbed into Songhai

● *Askia Muhammad*

● *Ibn Battuta visits Mali's capital*

● *Leo Africanus visits Timbuktu*

● *Moroccan armies overthrow Songhai, upset Sahara trade patterns*

France occupies the Western Sudan

Rise of Bornu dynasty

● *Ibn Fartua chronicles the reign of Mai Idris Alooma*

ASHANTI

● *King Osei Tutu unites weak forest states*

Ashanti dominates nearby peoples

British annexation ●

BENIN

Bronze-casting brought from Ife

● *João d'Aveiro visits Benin*

● *Ewuare the Great*

Dutch, Portuguese and English traders visit Benin

British annexation ●

YORUBA

State of Oyo reaches peak of power

Slave raids divide and weaken Yoruba peoples

British annexation ●

KONGO

Kongo founded by Bakongo warriors

● *King Afonso I*

● *Portuguese reach the Congo River*

Kongo disintegrates after antislavery wars

Belgian annexation ●

KILWA

● *Ibn Battuta visits Kilwa*

Pedro Cabral arrives with Portuguese fleet ●

● *Portuguese sack Kilwa, build Gereza fortress*

● *Zimba peoples destroy Kilwa*

ZIMBABWE

● *King Mutota conquers neighboring tribes*

Great Temple

Nguni tribesmen overrun Zimbabwe

BUGANDA

Lwo peoples occupy Uganda

Lwo Bunyoro kingdom dominates Lakes region

Buganda subkingdom takes over Bunyoro territories, develops as a strong central state

H. M. Stanley visits King Mutesa ●

BIBLIOGRAPHY

These books were selected during the preparation of this volume for their interest and 'authority, and for their usefulness to readers seeking additional information on specific points. An asterisk (*) marks works available in both hardcover and paperback editions; a dagger (†) indicates availability only in paperback.

GEOGRAPHY

Brown, Leslie, *Africa: A Natural History*. Random House, 1960.
†Fordham, Paul, *The Geography of African Affairs*. Penguin Books, 1965.
Schulthess, Emil, *Africa*. Simon & Schuster, 1958

GENERAL HISTORY

Ady, P. H., *Regional Economic Atlas: Africa*. Clarendon Press, Oxford, 1965.
Blake, John William, *Europeans in West Africa, 1450-1560*. 2 vols. Hakluyt Society, 1942.
*Bohannan, Paul, *Africa and Africans*. Doubleday, 1964.
Bovill, E. W., *The Golden Trade of the Moors*. Oxford University Press, 1958.
Budge, E. A. Wallis, *A History of Ethiopia*, 2 vols. Methuen & Co., Ltd., 1928.
Curtin, Philip D., *The Image of Africa*. University of Wisconsin Press, 1964.
Davidson, Basil, *The African Past*. Little, Brown and Co., 1964.
Davidson, Basil, *Black Mother: The Years of the African Slave Trade*. Little, Brown and Co., 1961.
Davidson, Basil, *The Lost Cities of Africa*. Little, Brown and Co., 1959.
*Davidson, Basil, *Which Way Africa?* Peter Smith, 1964.
Dike, K. O., *Trade and Politics in the Niger Delta, 1830-85*. Oxford University Press, 1956.
Fage, J. D., *An Introduction to the History of West Africa*. Cambridge University Press, 1964.
Freeman-Grenville, G.S.P., ed., *The East African Coast: Select Documents from the First to the Earlier Nineteenth Century*. Clarendon Press, Oxford, 1962.
Fyfe, Christopher, *Sierra Leone Inheritance*. Oxford University Press, 1964.
Hodgkin, Thomas, ed., *Nigerian Perspectives*. Oxford University Press, 1960.
Jones, A.H.M., and Elizabeth Monroe, *A History of Ethiopia*. Oxford University Press, 1955.
Oliver, Roland, and Gervase Mathew, eds., *History of East Africa*. Vol. I. Oxford University Press, 1963.
*Oliver, Roland, and J. D. Fage, *A Short History of Africa*. New York University Press, 1963.
Oliver, Roland, and J. D. Fage, eds., *The Journal of African History*. 6 vols. Cambridge University Press, 1960-1965.
Rotberg, Robert I., *A Political History of Tropical Africa*. Harcourt, Brace & World, 1965.
Rotberg, Robert I., *The Rise of Nationalism in Central Africa*. Harvard University Press, 1965.
Shinnie, Margaret, *Ancient African Kingdoms*. St. Martin's Press, 1966.
Wolfson, Freda, *Pageant of Ghana*. Oxford University Press, 1958.

ANTHROPOLOGY AND SOCIOLOGY

Elias, T. O., *The Nature of African Customary Law*. Oxford University Press, 1956.
Evans-Pritchard, E. E., *Essays in Social Anthropology*. The Macmillan Co., 1963.
†Fortes, Meyer, and E. E. Evans-Pritchard, eds., *African Political Systems*. Oxford University Press, 1966.
*Miner, Horace, *The Primitive City of Timbuctoo*. American Philosophical Society, 1953.

Ottenberg, Simon and Phoebe, eds., *Cultures and Societies of Africa*. Random House, 1960.
Van Velsen, J., *The Politics of Kinship*. Humanities Press, 1964.
*Wilson, Monica, ed., *Good Company: a Study of Nyakyusa Age-Villages*. Peter Smith, 1951.

ART AND ARCHEOLOGY

Arkell, Anthony J., *A History of the Sudan to 1821*. Oxford University Press, 1961.
Bacon, Edward, ed., *Vanished Civilizations*. McGraw-Hill, 1963.
Carrington, J. F., *Talking Drums of Africa* The Kingsgate Press, 1949.
†Clark, J. Desmond, *The Prehistory of Southern Africa*. Penguin Books, 1959.
Elisofon, Eliot, and William Fagg, *The Sculpture of Africa*. Frederick A. Praeger, 1958.
Fagan, Brian, *Southern Africa*. Frederick A. Praeger, 1965.
Fagg, William, *Nigerian Images*. Frederick A. Praeger, 1963.
Fagg, William, *Tribes and Forms in African Art*. Tudor, 1965.
†Fagg, William, and Margaret Plass, *African Sculpture*. Dutton, 1964.
Fraser, Douglas, *Primitive Art*. Doubleday, 1962.
Kirkman, James S., *Men and Monuments on the East African Coast*. Lutterworth Press, 1964.
Kyerematen, A.A.Y., *Panoply of Ghana*. Frederick A. Praeger, 1964.
Leuzinger, Elsy, *The Art of Africa*. Crown Publishers, 1960.
Lhote, Henri, *The Search for the Tassili Frescoes: The Story of the Prehistoric Rock-Paintings of the Sahara*. Transl. by Alan H. Broderick. E. P. Dutton & Co., 1959.
Paulme, Denise, *African Sculpture*. Viking Press, 1962.
Radin, Paul, and James Johnson Sweeney, eds., *African Folktales and Sculpture*. Pantheon Books, 1964.
Trowell, Margaret, *Classical African Sculpture*. Frederick A. Praeger, 1964.
*Turnbull, Colin M., *The Forest People*. Simon & Schuster, 1961.
*Wingert, Paul S., *Primitive Art, Its Traditions and Styles*, Oxford University Press, 1962.

RELIGION AND PHILOSOPHY

†Forde, Daryll, ed., *African Worlds*. Oxford University Press, 1954.
†Howells, William White, *The Heathens*. Doubleday, 1963.
Idowu, E. B., *Olodumare: God in Yoruba Belief*. Frederick A. Praeger, 1963.
Lienhardt, Godfrey, *Divinity and Experience: The Religion of the Dinka*. Oxford University Press, 1961.
†Parrinder, E. Geoffrey, *African Traditional Religion*. Hutchinson's University Library, London, 1954.
Parrinder, E. Geoffrey, *West African Religion*. The Epworth Press, London, 1961.
Rotberg, Robert I., *Christian Missionaries and the Creation of Northern Rhodesia, 1880-1924*. Princeton University Press, 1965.
Trimingham, J. Spencer, *A History of Islam in West Africa*. Oxford University Press, 1962.
Trimingham, J. Spencer, *Islam in Ethiopia*. Barnes & Noble, 1965
Trimingham, J. Spencer, *Islam in the Sudan*. Barnes & Noble, 1965.

ART INFORMATION AND PICTURE CREDITS

The sources for the illustrations in this book are set forth below. Descriptive notes on the works of art are included. Credits for pictures positioned from left to right are separated by semicolons, from top to bottom by dashes. Photographers' names which follow a descriptive note appear in parentheses. Abbreviations include "c." for century and "ca." for circa.

(NOTE: Figures, masks and other art objects made of wood are not dated in the list below because of lack of accurate records. However, it may be assumed that none of these objects is more than 150 years old: due to destruction by insects and weather, few wooden artifacts last in their native surroundings more than 20 or 30 years, and it is only in the last century that great care has been taken to preserve them. Nevertheless, most of this African sculpture, though relatively recent, reflects traditions of art and craftsmanship that go back several centuries.)

Cover—The Oba of Benin and his court, from Nigeria, bronze plaque, ca. 1600, British Museum, London (Arnold Newman). 10-11—Glacier icefall in Ruwenzori Range, Congo-Uganda border (Emil Schulthess from Black Star); south flank of Mount Kahusi in Congo (Kinshasa) (E. S. Ross)—view of dunes in Central Sahara (Helfried Weyer). 12-13—Hut village in Lama-Kara region of Togo (Marc and Evelyne Bernheim from Rapho Guillumette). 14-15—Ruins of Meroitic pyramids in Sudan (Marc and Evelyne Bernheim from Rapho Guillumette).

CHAPTER 1: 16—Queen Mother of Benin from Nigeria, bronze sculpture, 16th c., University Museum, Philadelphia (Arnold Newman). 20-21—Drawings by Lowell Hess. 23—Title page from "Description et récit Historial du Riche Royaume d'or de Gunea" by Pieter de Marees, Amsterdam, 1605, Rare Book Division, New York Public Library. 24-31—Drawings by Leo and Diane Dillon.

CHAPTER 2: 32—Meroitic site of Musawwarat es Safra in Sudan, built 1st c. A.D. (Marc and Evelyne Bernheim from Rapho Guillumette). 38-39—Frieze from Meroitic Musawwarat es Safra site in Sudan (Marc and Evelyne Bernheim from Rapho Guillumette). 40—Slab from refectory floor of Monastery of Apa Jeremias, Sakkarah, Egypt, marble, 6th c. A.D., Coptic Museum, Cairo (Werner Forman). 41—Nubian Queen Mother Martha protected by Madonna and Child, fresco, ca. 10th c. A.D., Khartoum Museum, Sudan (Marc and Evelyne Bernheim from Rapho Guillumette). 43—View from the "Shelter of Horses," Tassili n'Ajjer Range, Algeria, photograph by Mission Henri Lhote. 44-57—Original renderings of rock paintings by Mission Henri Lhote, photographed at Musée de l'Homme, Paris (Erich Lessing from Magnum), 44-45—Hares from Period of Hunter, ca. 4500 B.C.; oxen from Period of pre-Herder, ca. 4000 B.C.—elephants from Period of Herder, ca. 3500 B.C.; giraffe from Period of Horse, ca. 1500 to 600 B.C.—camel with rider from Period of Camel, ca. 600 B.C. to 1000 A.D. 46-47—Dancing figures from Period of Hunter, ca. 6000 to 4000

B.C.—men with sheep from Period of Herder, ca. 3000-2500 B.C. 48-49—Camp scene from Period of Herder, ca. 3500-3000 B.C.; well scene from Period of Horse, ca. 1000 B.C.—women gathering grain from Period of Herder, ca. 4000-1500 B.C. 50-51—Musical scene from Period of Horse, ca. 800-700 B.C.—processional dance from Period of Hunter, 6000 to 4000 B.C. 52-53—Seated woman from Period of Herder, ca. 3500-3000 B.C.; women riding cattle from Period of Herder, ca. 4000 to 1500 B.C. 54-55—War scene from Period of Herder, ca. 3000-2500 B.C.—women with burrowing sticks from Period of Herder, ca. 3500-3000 B.C. 56-57—Trial scene from Period of Herder, ca. 4000-1500 B.C.

CHAPTER 3: 58—Ashanti blacksmith, Ghana (Larry Burrows). 61—Conical tower of Zimbabwe, Rhodesia (Mitsuo Nitta); drawing by Nicholas Fasciano, courtesy National Museums of Rhodesia. 62—Wall detail from Zimbabwe, Rhodesia, photograph courtesy Rhodesia National Tourist Board—wall detail from Naletale ruins, Rhodesia, photograph courtesy Central African Airways—wall detail from Naletale ruins, Rhodesia, photograph courtesy Central African Airways. 64-65—Drawings by Nicholas Fasciano from James Walton, *African Village*, J. L. Van Schaik Ltd., Pretoria, 1956, after diagram by Siegfried Frederick Nadel. 67-77—Photographs by Leni Riefenstahl.

CHAPTER 4: 78—Arab camel rider, illumination from *Maqamat* manuscript by Hariri, ink and color on paper, Baghdad, 1237, Bibliothèque Nationale, Paris, photograph courtesy American Heritage. 83—Copper ingot from Congo (Kinshasa), photograph courtesy Royal Museum of Central Africa, Brussels; spearhead currency from Congo (Kinshasa), photograph courtesy Royal Museum of Central Africa, Brussels; iron manilla from Ghana, photograph courtesy Chase Manhattan Bank Money Museum—iron chain from Uganda (Marc and Evelyne Bernheim from Rapho Guillumette) courtesy Uganda National Museum; circlet of cowrie shells from Uganda (Marc and Evelyne Bernheim from Rapho Guillumette) courtesy Uganda National Museum; bifurcated iron spear from Uganda (Marc and Evelyne Bernheim from Rapho Guillumette) courtesy Uganda National Museum. 86-87—Elephant tusks in Dar-es-Salaam, Tanzania (Marc and Evelyne Bernheim from Rapho Guillumette); gold coins from North Africa, photograph courtesy American Numismatic Society; salt from Bilma mines in Niger (Maurice Fiévet); *The Tribute Giraffe with Attendant* by Shen Tu, ink and color on silk, 1414, courtesy Ralph M. Chait Galleries, New York. 89—The King of Mali, detail from facsimile of Catalan Atlas by Abraham Cresques, colored ink on parchment, 1375, British Museum, London (R. B. Fleming). 92-93—View of Djanet, Algeria (Victor Englebert); camel caravan in Niger (Victor Englebert). 94-95—Two views of Lamu Island off Kenya coast (Lynn Millar from Rapho Guillumette). 96—Salt pits of Tegguida N'Tisemt in Niger (Afrique Photo, Cliché Naud, Paris). 97—View of Bilma oasis in Niger (Victor Englebert)—salt blocks of Fort Lamy in Chad (Afrique Photo, Cliché Naud, Paris). 98-99—Grain market at Marrakech, Morocco (Douglas Faulkner)—animal market at Goulimine, Morocco (Douglas Faulkner).

CHAPTER 5: 100—The Oba of Benin, Nigeria (Dr. R. E. Bradbury). 102-103—Culver Pictures. 105—Copper engraving by unknown artist, German, 15th c. (Bettmann Archive). 106—Man on horse, Ashanti goldweight from Ghana, brass, collection of Chaim Gross, New York (Eliot Elisofon). 109—Royal gateway of Benin, Nigeria, bronze plaque, 16th or 17th c., British Museum, London (Werner Forman). 110-111—Armed warriors and Oba of Benin with attendants, Nigeria, bronze plaques, late 17th or early 18th c., British Museum, London (Arnold Newman); Queen Mother of Benin with attendants, Nigeria, bronze sculpture, late 18th or early 19th c., Staatliche Museen zu Berlin, Museum für Völkerkunde (Werner Forman). 112-113—Slit-gong player from Benin, Nigeria, bronze plaque 16th or 17th c., British Museum, London (Werner Forman); acrobats from Benin, Nigeria, bronze plaque, late 16th c., British Museum, London (Werner Forman). 114-115—Leopard hunters from Benin, Nigeria, bronze plaque, late 16th or early 17th c., Staatliche Museen zu Berlin, Museum für Völkerkunde (Werner Forman); hunter shooting ibis, Benin, Nigeria, bronze plaque, 16th c., British Museum, London (Werner Forman). 116-117—Man with box, Nigeria, bronze plaque, 16th or 17th c., British Museum, London (Werner Forman); visitor to Benin, Nigeria, bronze sculpture, late 18th c., British Museum, London (Werner Forman); Benin merchant holding manilla, Nigeria, bronze plaque, early 17th c., British Museum, London (Werner Forman). 118-119—Warrior from Benin, Nigeria, bronze plaque, late 16th c., Staatliche Museen zu Berlin, Museum für Völkerkunde (Werner Forman); battle scene, Nigeria, late 16th c., Staatliches Museum für Völkerkunde, Dresden (Werner Forman).

CHAPTER 6: 120—Increase fetish from Baluba, Congo, wood, calabash, and snail shells, collection of Tristan Tzara, Paris (Eliot Elisofon). 122—Gaboon viper from Guinea, painted wood, collection of Armand Bartos, New York (Eliot Elisofon). 123—Nail-fetish figure from Congo (Brazzaville), Loango tribe, wood and iron, Musée de l'Homme, Paris (Eliot Elisofon). 124-Mouse oracle from Ivory Coast, Baule tribe, wood, Musée de l'Homme, Paris (Eliot Elisofon). 127-Congolese boys in ritual masks, Bayaka tribe (Eliot Elisofon). 129—Life-sized stone relief of St. George, Church of Golgotha-Mikael in Lalibela, Ethiopia, red volcanic tuff, 13th c. (Dr. Georg Gerster from Rapho Guillumette). 130-131—Three illuminations from 19th c. manuscript *The Life of St. Lalibela:* "The making of the covenant between God and King Lalibela"; "Building the Church of St. Mary"—"The buildings of Lalibela," British Museum, London (Derek Bayes). 132-133—Three views of Church of St. George in form of Greek cross, Lalibela, Ethiopia, red volcanic tuff, 13th c. (Dr. Georg Gerster from Rapho Guillumette). 134-135—Window details from Lalibela churches: Church of St. Mary; Church of Abba Libanos; Church of Saint Mascal—Church of Golgotha-Mikael; Church of Golgotha-Mikael; Church of St. Mary, carved red volcanic tuff, 13th c. (Dr. Georg Gerster from Rapho Guillumette). 136-137—Interior scenes of columns and vaults of Lalibela churches: Church of St. Mary; Church of the Savior of the World; Church of St. Mary, carved and painted red volcanic tuff, 13th c. (Dr. Georg Gerster from Rapho Guillumette). 138-139—Composite scene of *Jesus and the Samaritan Woman* and *Jesus and the Man Disabled 38 Years*, painted on wall of Church of St. Mary, 13th c. (Dr. Georg Gerster from Rapho Guillumette)—Scene variously interpreted as *Shadrach, Meshach and Abednego* or *Kings Christos, Lalibela and Naakuto-Laab*, painted on wall of Church of St. Merkurios, 13th c. (Dr. Georg Gerster from Rapho Guillumette). 140-141—Crypt in Church of Golgotha-Mikael, red volcanic tuff, 13th c. (Dr. Georg Gerster from Rapho Guillumette).

CHAPTER 7: 142—Door to secret-society shrine, from Ivory Coast, Senufo tribe, wood, University Museum, Philadelphia (Eliot Elisofon). 144—Stone head of a woman by Amedeo Modigliani, Paris, 1912, collection of Baron Boël, Brussels, photograph from Alfred Werner, *Modigliani the Sculptor*, Arts Inc., New York, 1962. 145—Dance mask from Gabon, Fang tribe, painted wood, collection of Pierre Verité, Paris (Eliot Elisofon). 146—Head from Nigeria (Nok), terra cotta, ca. 2nd or 1st c. B.C., Jos Museum, Nigeria (Eliot Elisofon); memorial head from Nigeria (Ife), brass, 13th c. A.D., Ife Museum, Nigeria (Eliot Elisofon). 147—Head from Nigeria (Benin), bronze and iron, ca. 1650, Museum of Primitive Art, New York (Charles Uht). 149—Drawing and notation by Nicholas Fasciano in consultation with Nicholas M. England, Columbia University, and Bertram Buckner. 151-165—Photographs by Eliot Elisofon. 151—Female figure, detail of heddle pulley from Ivory Coast, Guro tribe, wood, collection of Harold Rome, New York. 152-153—Three views of ancestor figure from Mali, Dogon tribe, wood, Elisofon Collection; akua'ba doll from Ghana, Ashanti, wood, Elisofon Collection; man on horse from Mali, Bambara tribe, iron, Elisofon Collection; two views of rhythm pounder from Ivory Coast, Senufo tribe, wood, Elisofon Collection. 154—Details from two cosmetic boxes from Congo (Kinshasa), Bushongo tribe, wood, Elisofon Collection. 155—Detail of heddle pulley from Ivory Coast, Baule tribe, wood, collection of Harold Rome, New York. 156-157—Eight heddle pulleys in silhouette from Ivory Coast, Guro tribe, wood, collection of Harold Rome, New York. 158—Detail of ancestor figure from Congo (Kinshasa), Bena Lulua tribe, wood, Elisofon Collection. 159—Reliquary figure from Gabon, Fang tribe, wood, Elisofon Collection. 160-161—Seven ritual masks, all wood: from Ivory Coast, Baule tribe; from Mali, Bambara tribe—from Mali, Bambara tribe; from Cameroon, Grassland tribes; from Congo (Kinshasa), Basonge tribe; from Upper Volta, Bobo tribe; from Ivory Coast-Liberia region, Ngere-Dan tribe, Elisofon Collection. 162-163—Cup for palm wine from Congo (Kinshasa), Bushongo tribe, wood, Elisofon Collection; knife from Congo (Kinshasa)-Sudan region, Azande tribe, iron, Elisofon Collection; stool from Mali, Bambara tribe, wood, Elisofon Collection; spoon from Mali, Bambara tribe, wood, Elisofon Collection; headrest from Mali, Dogon tribe, wood, collection of Harold Rome, New York—headrest from Rhodesia, Mashona tribe, wood, collection of Harold Rome, New York. 164-165—Ancestor figure from Mali, Dogon tribe, wood, Elisofon Collection.

CHAPTER 8: 166—Portion of map by Juan de la Cosa, 1500, facsimile, British Museum, London (Alan Clifton). 170-171—The King of Kongo, illustration from *Umbständliche und Eigentliche Beschreibung von Afrika*, by Oliver Dapper, Amsterdam, 1670 (New York Public Library). 175—Hut in Cameroon (Peter Larsen from Nancy Palmer Photo Agency). 176-177—Village in Chad, photograph courtesy Editions Hoa-Qui, Paris; house in Kano, Nigeria (Klaus Paysan)—Dinka huts in Sudan (Klaus Paysan). 178-179—Great temple at Zimbabwe, Rhodesia (D. Attenborough); the parallel passage at Zimbabwe, Rhodesia (Terence Spencer from Black Star). 180-181—Two views of Great Mosque at Kilwa, Tanzania (Marc and Evelyne Bernheim from Rapho Guillumette). 182-183—Gereza Fortress, Kilwa, Tanzania (Marc and Evelyne Bernheim from Rapho Guillumette).

ACKNOWLEDGMENTS

The editors of this book are particularly indebted to Robert I. Rotberg, Assistant Professor of History, Harvard University, and the following individuals and institutions: UNITED STATES: Eliot Elisofon, New York; Nicholas M. England, Center for Studies in Ethnomusicology, Columbia University: Margaret Plass, Curator of African Art, University Museum, University of Pennsylvania; Lloyd Cabot Briggs, Research Fellow in North African Anthropology, Peabody Museum, Harvard University; Leslie Elam, Editor, American Numismatic Society, New York; Harold Rome, New York; John B. Schmitt, Professor of Entomology, Rutgers University; Victor Englebert, New York; Gerard Alexander, Chief of Map Division, New York Public Library; Matila Simon, New York. EUROPE: William Fagg, Deputy Keeper, Department of Ethnography, British Museum, London; School of Oriental and African Studies, University of London; Dr. R. E. Bradbury, Centre of West African Studies, University of Birmingham; Raymond Mauny, Professor of Tropical African History, University of Paris; Jean Leclant, Professor of Egyptology, University of Paris; Henri Lhote, Chief of Research, National Center for Scientific Research, Paris; André Caquot, Director, Section of Religious Sciences, Ecole Pratique des Hautes Etudes, University of Paris; Bertrand de Saboulin Bollena, Deputy Director, Compagnie des Salins du Midi et des Salines de Djibouti, Paris; Dr. Kurt Krieger, Museum für Völkerkunde, Berlin; Fritz Hintze, Professor of Egyptology, Humboldt University, East Berlin; Dr. S. Wolf, Staatliches Museum für Völkerkunde, Dresden; Antonio Mordini, Barga, Lucca Province, Italy. AFRICA: Richard Pankhurst, Director, Institute of Ethiopian Studies, Addis Ababa; Roland C. Stevenson, Linguistic Consultant, Nairobi; H. Neville Chittick, Director, and Brian Fagan, British Institute of History and Archaeology in East Africa, Nairobi; James S. Kirkman, Keeper, Kenya National Museum, Fort Jesus, Mombasa; Vincent Monteil, Director, Institut Fondamental d'Afrique Noire, Dakar.

INDEX

*This symbol in front of a page number indicates a photograph or painting of the subject mentioned.

MAPS IN THIS VOLUME

All maps by David Greenspan

The Topography of Africa	8-9
Africa and the U.S.: A Comparison	19
The Nile Valley	34
Trading Empires	81
Trade Routes	90-91

A

Abiri, Ife tomb at, 147
Aden, *map* 91
Aden, Gulf of, *map* 9
Administration: Ashanti, 108; Benin, 104, 109, 111; role of "secret societies," 126-127; Western Sudanese kingdoms, 85, 103. *See also* Law and order
Adulis, 41, 42, *map* 91
African character and values, 19, 21-22, 60-66, 174; attitudes toward war, 64-65; morality, 22, 42, 64; nonmaterialist attitudes, 22, 60; sense of justice, 82-83; traditionalism, 143, 145, 148, 169-170, 172-174
Age patterns, in social organization, 63-64
Agriculture, 21, 169; Dinka, 63; Sahara, Stone Age, 19, 46, 48, *49; tropical, 22; various products of, 170, 171
Ahaggar Mountains, *map* 8
Al-Andalusi, Abu Hamid, 81
Al-Bakri of Córdoba, 80, 82, 83
Alexandria, Egypt, *map* 8, *map* 90-91; center of Christianity, 42, 129
Algiers, *map* 90
Al-Kati, Mahmud, 79-80
Almaqah, god, 41
Al-Masudi, 61
Alodia, Kingdom of, 39, 40
Alvares, Francisco, 129
Amenophis I, King of Egypt, 35
American Indians, social behavior compared with African, 60
Americas, African contributions in: cultural, 168-169; economic, 168
Amon, god, 35
Amulets, 125
Ananse Kokrofo, Great Spider, 150
Ancestor figures, *152, *164-165
Ancestor worship, *122, 126-127, 128
Angola, 104, 171; slave trade, 105
Animal husbandry, 21, 171; Dinka, 62-63; Sahara, 19, 44, 46, *48-49, 52
Animal market, *98-99
Animals: in African art, 37, *38-39, *44-49, *53, *142, 147, 148, *160-161; as beasts of burden, 46, *78, 81, 89, *map* 90-91, *92-93, *97; in religion, 37, 121, *122, *142; sacrifice of, *46-47, 63, *76-77, 122
Anopheles mosquito, *20
Anthropology, 19, 22
Antioch, 42
Aquinas, Thomas, 105
Arabia: East African trade of, 87, 88; Ethiopian trade with, 41, 42; Kushite trade with, 37
Arabs: conquest of North Africa, 81; East African slave trade of, 170; in Egypt, 40; traders, *78, *89. *See also* Muslims
Archeological excavations and exploration, 18, 22; at Ife, 145; at Kilwa, 88; in Kush, 36, 37; in Mauritania, 80; in

Nigeria, 145, 146, 147-148; in Nubia, 39; in Sahara, 19, *43-57; at Zimbabwe, 178
Architecture, 175; Egyptian pyramids, 34; Ethiopian, 42, 129, 131, *132-137, *140-141; Ghana, 80; Kilwa, 88, *180-181; Kushite, *14-15, *32, 36, 37; Naletale, *62; Zimbabwe, 59, *61, *62, 88, *178-179. *See also* Building materials; Churches; Housing; Mosques; Palaces; Pyramids; Temples
Area of African continent, *map* 19
Armor, Ashanti, *106; Bini, *110, *118-119; Bornu, *30-31. *See also* Weapons
Art: chief characteristics of, 143; court, 147 (*see also* Benin, sculpture of; Ife, sculpture of); form, 143; geometrical, 145, 148, *154-155; initial European misjudgment as "primitive," 143-146; of present, 150; religious basis of, 143, 145, 147, 148, 150, 151, 153, 160; style, 143; traditionalism in, 143, 145, 148, *156-157; Western, African impact on, *144-145, 150, 165. *See also* Architecture; Dance; Music; Painting; Sculpture; Storytelling
Ashanti: blacksmiths, *58; Kingdom of, 107-108, 126, 172; religion of, 123-124, 125, 126; sculpture, 22, *106, *152; warrior, figurine, *106
Asiut, *map* 91
Askia the Great (Askia Muhammad Touré), King of Songhai, 79-80
Aspelta, King of Kush, 36
Assyria, conquest of Egypt by, 36
Aswan Dam, 39
Atlas Mountains, *map* 8
Awdoghast, 82, *map* 90
Axim, *map* 90, 91
Axum, *map* 9, 22, 38, 42, *map* 91

B

Bacon, Roger, 105
Baga people, snake worship, *122
Baker, Sir Samuel, 62
Baluba people, fetish, *120
Bamako, 80
Bambara people, sculpture of, 148
Bantu languages, 21
Baptista, Pedro João, 170-171
Barbosa, Duarte, 88
Barka, *map* 90
Barth, Heinrich, 172
Basonge mask, *160-161
Baule people: masks of, 144, *160-161; mouse oracle, *124
Bayaka initiation masks, *127
Belloc, Hilaire, 173
Benguela, *map* 90
Benin, Chief of, *100
Benin, city, *map* 8, 18, *map* 90, 101-102, 103-104, 109, 118
Benin, Bight of, *map* 8

Benin, Kingdom of, 101-102, 103-104, 109, 111, 112, 172; demise of, 108, 118; human sacrifice in, 108, 112, 118; hunting, *114-115; sculpture of, *16, 22, 103, *109-119, 144-145, *147; trade, 104-105, *116-117; warfare, *118-119
Benin chief, *100
Benue River, *map* 8
Berber culture, 20
Bible, 38
Bilma, oasis, *map* 90; salt mining near, *97
Bini, the, 109. *See also* Benin
Black Noba, 38, 41
Blacksmiths, Ashanti, *58
Blomert, Samuel, 104
Bonnel de Mézières, Albert, 80
Bonny, kingdom, 108
Book trade, Timbuktu, 17-18, 84
Bornu cavalry, *30-31
Bowdich, Thomas, 107-108
Braque, Georges, and African art, 165
Brass sculpture, *146
Brava, *map* 91
Brazil, African slave labor in, 168
British colonialism in West Africa, 108, 167-168
Brohimi, 173-174
Bronze plaques, Benin, 104, *109, 144-145, *147
Bronze sculpture, *16, 103, *109-119, 144, *147, 148
Bronze weapons, 36
Bruce, James, 39
Buhen, 35
Building materials, *62, 177, *178-180
Bulala people, *30-31
Burton, Sir Richard, 60
Bushmen, 20, 21
Bushongo tribe, geometrical art of, *154
Byzantium: cultural influence in Ethiopia, 134, 137, *138-139; Ethiopian trade with, 42

C

Cabral, Pedro Alvares, 88
Cadornega, 105
Cairo, *map* 9, 83, 84, *map* 91
Camel, as beast of burden, 46, *78, 81, 89, *map* 90-91, *92-93, *97
Camel period, Saharan peoples, 46
Cannibalism, myths, 18
Caravan routes, *map* 90-91, *92-93
Caravel routes, *map* 90-91
Caravels, Portuguese, *28, 91
Caribbean, African slave labor in, 168
Carthaginians, 37
Caseley Hayford, J. E., 168
Cattle. *See* Animal husbandry
Cavalry, Bornu, *30-31
Central Africa: Baptista's account of, 170-171; kingdoms of, 59-60, 88
Central Sudan, Bornu cavalry, *30-31
Ceremonies. *See* Festivals; Initiation ceremonies; Rituals
Césaire, Aimé, 22
Ceylon, Ethiopian trade with, 42
Chad, Lake, *map* 8, 37, 81, *map* 90; salt mining, *97
Chad village, *176-177
Chari River, *map* 8
Chief of Benin, *100
Chief's stool, *162
China: East African trade with, 87, 91; Kushite trade with, 37
Chittick, Neville, 88
Christianity, 121, 128; in Axum, 22, 42; "backsliding" of converts, 128; Coptic fresco, *41; Coptic prayer, *40; Coptics, 40, 42; early missionaries in Afri-

ca (Sixth Century), 39-40; in Ethiopia, 41, 42, *129-141; kingdoms in Nubia, 39-41
Churches, Ethiopian, 42, *129, 131, *132-141
Cities and towns, 21, 23, *map* 90-91; East African coast, 17, 18, *28-29, 88, 94, *180-181; Kushite, 36, 37, 39; West African coastal and forest regions, 18, 101-102, 103-104, 107-108, 109, 118; Western Sudanese kingdoms, 17-18, *24-27, 79, 80, 81, 82, 84, 85, 86
Clay sculpture, 145, *146, 147, 148
Climate, changes in, 19-20; desiccation of Sahara, 19-20, 36, 43, 46, 55
Clothing: in Kilwa, 88; Saharan herdsmen, in warfare, *54-55; Saharan peoples, *53, *56-57; of traders, 98, *99, 104
Coins, *86; Benin manilla, 116, *117; Ethiopian, 42; Kilwan, 88
Colonialism, European, 107, 108, 167-168, 169, 170
Columbus, Christopher, 85, 106
Congo: cultural similarities with Egypt, 34; precolonial, law and order in, 171; pygmies of, 61-62; religious fetishes and practices, *120, *127, 144; slave trade, 105
Congo River, *map* 9, *map* 90
Conservatism. *See* Traditionalism
Copper: trade, 88; use of, 36
Coptic Christians, 40, 42; fresco, *41; prayer, *40
Cotton-weaving industry, Kano, 172-173
Crafts, *154-157, *162-163, 169, 173; Saharan peoples, 52
Creation, concept of, 124
Cresques, Abraham, 84-85
Crusades, medieval, 40
Cubism, 165
Currencies, 42, 82, *83, *86, 88, 106, 116, *117

D

D'Abbadie, brothers, 42
Da Gama, Vasco, 17, 18, 42
Dan people, masks of, 144
Dance, 143, 146, 148, 150, 160; Benin, *113; costumes and masks, *127, 144, 150, *160-161; Saharan Stone Age peoples, *50-51
Dapper, Olfert, 104
Darfur, *map* 9, *map* 90
D'Aveiro, João Affonso, 102
Dei, Benedetto, 24, 85
Derain, André, and African art, 165
Desert travel, *78, 81-82, *map* 90-91, *92-93
Deserts, *map* 8-9, *10-11, 20. *See also* Sahara Desert
Dhow routes, *map* 90-91
Dhows, *28-29, 91, *94-95
Dinka, 62-63, 172; hut, *177; religion of, 123-124; social organization of, 62-63, 169
Diseases, 20; insect carriers, *20-21
Djanet, oasis, *92
Dog, domestication of, 49
Dogon sculpture, *152, *164-165
Dongola, *map* 91
Donkey, as beast of burden, 89, *map* 90-91
Drakensberg Mountains, *map* 9
Drummond, Henry, 60
Drums and drumming, 146, 148-150; Yoruba, *149
Dutch traders, 102, 107, *171; descriptions of Africa by, 18, 23, 103-104

E

East Africa: anthropological fossil finds, 19; cities of, 17, 18, *28-29, 88, map 91, 94, *180-181; slave trade, 87, 170, 180; trade, *28-29, 37, 41, 86, 87-88, map 91, *94-95, 105, 180
Ed-Dukkali, Sheik Uthman, 84
Education: African religious, 125-126, 127; by European missionaries, 66; Western Sudanese merchant cities, 18, 24, 80, 82, 84
Egypt, ancient, 20; Assyrians in, 36; cultural interaction with rest of Africa, 34-35; dynastic times, 34-35; early kingdoms of, 33-34; Ethiopian trade with, 41; expansion into Nubia and Sudan, 35; under Fatimid rulers, 40; under Kushite control, 35-36; Kushite trade with, 37; Libyan princes of, 20; Islamization of, 40, 129; political decline of, 35; under Saracen rulers, 40; unification of, 34
Ehengbuda, King of Benin, 104
Eighteenth Dynasty, Egypt, 35
Elephants: in African art, 37, *44-45; hunting of, *115; use in warfare and ceremonies, 37, *38-39
Elisofon, Eliot, 151; photographs of African sculpture by, *151-165
Elizabeth I, Queen of England, 86
Elmina, map 90, 91, 101
Empires. See Kingdoms and empires
English traders, 86, 102-103, 107; descriptions of Africa by, 102, 103, 107-108
Equiano, Olaudah, 170, 171
Ergamenes, King of Kush, 37
Esarhaddon, King of Assyria, 36
Esie, stone sculpture finds at, 147-148
Ethiopia: ancient Greek references to, meaning Kush, 36; Christianity in, 41, 42, 129, 140-141; churches of, 42, *129, 131, *132-141; civilization of, 41-42; ethnic composition, 139; history of, 41-42, 131, 139; invasion of Kush by, 38-39; legend, 41, 131, 132, 139; Portuguese in, 42, 129; Solomonid dynasty of (Lion of Judah), 41, 131, 139; trade, 41, 42, 134; Zagwe dynasty of, 131, 139
Ethiopian Highlands, map 9
Europe: colonialism of, 107, 108, 167-168, 169, 170; crusades, 40; medieval and post-medieval, comparisons with Africa, 21, 42, 60-61, *105, 122, 127, 128, 143; need for gold, 22, 86; in North and West African trade, *23, 84-85, 86, 91, 101, 102-103, 104-107; occultism in, *105, 127; political relations with West African kingdoms, around 1500, 101-102; and slave trade, 105-107
European concepts of Africa, 17-18, 21-22, 122, 143-144; around 1500, 21, 103, map 166; misjudgment of art as "primitive," 143-146; myths, 18; 19th Century, 22, 59-60, 62, 64, 167
Evans-Pritchard, E. E., 64-65
Ewuare the Great, King of Benin, 103
Excavations, 19. See also Archeological excavations
Ezana, King of Ethiopia, 38, 41, 42

F

Fagg, Bernard, 146
Fang tribe, ritual mask of, *145
Faras, 39
Farming. See Agriculture
Fatimids, in Egypt, 40
Ferrer, Jacme, 84
Fertile plains, map 8-9, *14-15
Fertility fetish, *120
Fertility symbols, animal, *142
Festivals: Benin, *112-113; and dance, 148
Fetish worship, 122
Fetishes, *120, *122-123
Feudalism, in Ethiopia, 42
Fez, map 8, map 90
Florence, and African trade, 84, 85
Folk tales, 150

Food, 21, 170; Nuba, 65; Songhai, 85
Forests, map 8-9, *10-11, 20
Fortes, Meyer, 65
Fossils, anthropological, 19
Fourth Dynasty, Egypt, 34, 35
French trade with West Africa, 102
Frobenius, Leo, 144
Funeral, Nuba, *74-77
Funerary figure, *159

G

Gabon, 104
Gambia River, map 8, map 90
Gamitto, Antonio Candido, 171-172
Ganda, kingdom of the, 172
Gao, map 8, 86, map 90, 91; description by Leo Africanus, 85
Garamantes people, 55
Geez language, 42, 138
Genoa, and African trade, 84, 85
Geography of Africa, map 8-9, *10-15, map 19
Gereza fortress, Kilwa, *182-183
Ghadames, map 90, 91
Ghana, Kingdom of, 80, map 81, 82, 83, 86-87; civilization of, 81; dates of existence of, 81; trade, 81-82
Ghana, region of: Ashanti of, 107-108, 123-124, 126; Tallensi of, 65-66, 126
Ghana, Republic of, 87. See also Gold Coast
Ghat, map 8, map 90
Ghiarou, map 90
Gizeh, pyramids of, 34
Goats, domestication, 46
Gods, 123-126; High God, 123-124; lesser, 124, 125-126
Gol, social unit of Dinka, 63
Gold: basis of wealth and power of West African kingdoms, 80, 81, 83-84, 86-87, 89; coins, *86; East African trade in, 29, 86, 87, 88, map 91, 94; Europe's demand for, 22, 86; mining, 87, map 90-91; in North and West African trade, 81-82, 85, 86-87, 89, map 90, 91, 106, 107; sources, 86-87, 107
Gold Coast, map 90; encounter of Europeans with natives, *23, 101; trade, 104-105
Golden Stool of Osei Tutu, 107, 126
Gondar, map 91
Good Hope, Cape of, map 9
Goulimine, animal market, *98-99
Grasslands, map 8-9, *12-13, 19, 20; Western Sudan, empires of, 80-81
Great Mosque, Kilwa, *180-181
Great Temple, Zimbabwe, 59, *61, *62, 88, *178-179
Greeks, ancient, 33, 37; cultural influence in Ethiopia, 134, *135; references to Ethiopia meaning Kush, 36
Guangara, Kingdom of, 86
Guinea, Description of, Marees, 103-104
Guinea, Gulf of, map 8; trade, map 90, 91
Guinea, Republic of, 79, 87
Guinea coast, 102, 103, 127
Guinea Highlands, map 8
Guro sculpture, *151, *156-157

H

Fagg, Bernard, 146
Haile Selassie, Emperor of Ethiopia, 41, 168
Hair styles, *52-53
Hawkins, John, 102-103
Head porterage, 89, map 90-91
Headless people, myth of, 18
Heliodorus, 38
Herder period, Saharan peoples, 19, 46, *48-55; eclipse of, 55
Herodotus, 36, 55; quoted, 33
Hieroglyphs: Egyptian, 37; Meroitic, 37
High God, 123-124
History and Description of Africa, The, Leo Africanus, 85
Holy Roman Empire, 40
Horse, domestication of, 46
Horse period, Saharan peoples, 46, 55

Housing, *24-25, 36, *62, 80, 88, 104, 170. See also Huts
Howells, William, 122
Human sacrifice, 108, 112, 118
Hunter period, Saharan peoples, 19, 46
Hunting, 21, 46, 49, *114-115
Husuni Kubwa, palace, Kilwa, 88
Huts, *24-25, 36, *62, 80, 88, 104, 170, *58; Cameroon, *175; Chad, *176-177; Dinka, *177; Nigerian, *177; Nuban, mud, *64-65, *68-69; Saharan Herder period, wickerwork, 49

I

Ibn Battuta, 82-83, 88
Ibn Hawqal, 82
Iboland, 170, 171
Ife, map 8; sculpture, 103, 145, *146, 147
Immortality, belief in, 123, 128. See also Ancestor worship
Imperialism, European, 167. See also Colonialism
India: East African trade of, 87, 88, 91; Ethiopian trade with, 42; Kushite trade with, 37
Indian Ocean trade: East African, 87-88, 94, 105, 180; Ethiopian, 41, 42
Industry: beginnings of, in precolonial Africa, 108, 172-173; iron, Kushite, 37
Initiation ceremonies, 126, 160; Bayaka, 127; of Nuba wrestlers, *70-71; Sahara, Stone Age, *46-47
Initiation masks, *127, *160-161
Inventions, 22
Iron Age, coming of, 21, 36-37, 146
Iron: mining and working, Meroë, 37; trade, East Africa, 29, 37, 38; weapons, 21, 36; working, Ashanti, *58
Irtet, under Egyptian control, 35
Islam, 42, 103, 121, 128; in Egypt, 40, 129; in Nubia, 40-41; religious war in West Africa, 170; in Western Sudanese kingdoms, 27, 80, 82, 84, 103. See also Muslims
Italian city-states, and African trade, 84, 85
Ivory Coast, map 90, 107, 144
Ivory trade, 29, 42 *86, 87, 88, 91, 94, 102

J

Ja Ja, King of Opobo, 108
Jenne, 84, map 90
Jesus, the, 102-103
Jobson, Richard, 103
John Lackland, King of England, 60-61
John III, King of Portugal, 105
John of Ephesus, 39-40
José, Amaro, 170, 171
Jos, museum at, 146
Julian, missionary, 39-40, 42
Justice, sense of, 82-83. See also Law and order
Justinian, Roman Emperor, 40, 42

K

Kalahari Desert, map 9, map 90
Kanem-Bornu, Kingdom of, map 81. See also Bornu
Kanissa'ai, King of Ghana, 80
Kano, map 8, 86, map 90, 172
Kasai River, map 9, 171
Katanga, 171
Katsina, 86, map 90
Kazembe, Mwata, 171-172
Kemalke, 38
Kenya, historical reference to region of, 87
Khartoum, map 9
Kilwa, map 9, 22, 88, map 91, 94, 180; Great Mosque of, *180-181; harbor of, *28-29, 88; Portuguese fortress at, 175, *182-183
Kingdoms and empires, 22, 171-172; Ethiopia (Axum), 22, 41-42, 131, 139; Kush, 22, 35-38; Nubian, 39-40, *41; of

West African coastal and forest regions, 101-102, 103-105, 107-108, *109-119, 172 (see also Ashanti; Benin; Kanem-Bornu; Kongo; Oyo); of Western Sudan, 79-80, map 81, 82-84, 101, 103, 105, 172 (see also Ghana; Mali; Songhai); Zimbabwe, 22, 59-60, 66, 88, *178-179
Kings: divinity of, 34, 111; royal courts of West African, *26-27, 79, 80, 83, 85, 104, 107-108, *110-111
Kingsley, Mary, 167-168
Kinship patterns, 60, 63, 65, 66, 106
Kisimani-Mafia, 88
Kongo, Kingdom of, 101, 105, *171
Korongo, Nuba tribe, 67
Kosseir, map 91
Kota people: geometrical art of, 145, 148; masks of, 144
Kumasi, map 8, map 90, 107-108
Kumbi Salih, 80
Kush, Kingdom of, 22, 35-38, 103; architecture of, *14-15, *32, 36, 37, at of, *38-39; civilization of, 36-38, 39; decline of, 38; Egypt under control of, 35-36; under Egyptian control, 35; Egyptian influences in, 35, 37; Ethiopian invasion of, 38-39; main periods of history of, 35; Meroitic period, 35, 36-38; Napatan period, 35-36; trade, 37, 38

L

Lagos, island of, 173
Lake Tonga. See Tonga
Lalibela, King of Ethiopia, 42, 129, *130-131, 139, 141
Lalibela, town, map 9, 129; churches of, *129, 131, *132-141
Lamu, map 9, map 91, *94
Landscape, map 8-9, *10-15, 20
Languages: Bantu, 21; Geez, 42, 138; Swahili, 29
Law and order: Kingdom of Benin, 104; Kingdom of Mali, 82-83; Kingdom of the Ganda, 172; in precolonial Congo, Baptista's account of, 171; role of ancestor cult in, 126-127, 128; Saharan peoples, *56-57; Tallensi, 65-66
Lasta, mountains of, 42
Leo X, Pope, 17, 84, 86
Leo Africanus (Hassan Ibn Muhammad), 24, 79, 84, 86, 97; The History and Description of Africa, 85
Lhote, Henri, 43, 44, 45, 49, 51, 56
Libraries, Timbuktu, 84
Libya: nomads of, 35; settlement of, 20
Life-Force, religious concept, 123, 145, 146, 151
Limpopo River, map 9, 59
Lion, in religion, 37
Lion of Judah, Ethiopian dynasty, 41. See also Solomonid dynasty
Lion Temple, Musawwarat, frieze, *38-39
Lip ring, *74
Literacy: West African coastal region, 103, 107, 108; Western Sudanese kingdoms, 82, 103. See also Writing
Literature: Geez, 42; Islamic, Western Sudan, 84; oral, 150
Living standard, advanced African societies, 21, 169, 170-171
Livingstone, David, 66, 128, 170
Lloyd, A. B., 149
Locust, pest, *21
Luanda, map 90
Luapula River, 171

M

Madagascar, map 9, map 91
Magic, 127-128; charms, table 125; comparison with Europe, *105, 127, 128
Makuria, Kingdom of, 39, 40
Malaguetta, *103
Malaguetta (Pepper) Coast, map 90, 103
Malaria, 20, 21

Malawi, Lake (Lake Nyasa) *map* 9, 66, *map* 91; trading contacts, 88
Malequerebar, King of Kush, 38
Malfante, Antonio, 85
Mali, Kingdom of, 26, *map* 81, 82-84, 85, 87, 88; court ceremony, *26-27, 83; dates of existence of, 81; military power of, 101; salt mining, 97; trade, 81, 86, *89
Mali, Republic of, 79, 80
Malindi, *map* 9, 87, 88, *map* 91, 180
Manan, *map* 90
Manilla, coin, 116, *117
Mansa Musa. *See* Musa
Manuel, King of Portugal, 101, 105
Marees, Pieter de, 23, 103
Marketplaces, *98-99
Marrakech, *map* 8, *map* 90, 91; market, 98, *99
Marseilles, and African trade, 84, 85
Masks, 144, *145, 148, 150, *160-161; initiation, *127, 160
Matisse, Henri, and African art, 165
Mauch, Karl, 178
Mauny, Raymond, 80
Mauritania, historical reference to region of, 80
Mecca, *map* 9
Medicine, herbal, 125, 128
Mediterranean peoples and cultures, 20
Memphis, *map* 9; Kushite seizure of, 35-36
Menelik, King of Ethiopia, 41, 139
Menes, King of Egypt, 34
Meroë, *map* 9, *map* 34; Kushite capital, 35, 36-38
Mesakin, Nuba tribe, 67
Metals, 21, 22. *See also* Bronze; Copper; Gold; Iron; Mining
Migrations, 19, 20, 21, 107
Military power: Bornu, *30-31; West African kingdoms, 101, 107, 108, 118. *See also* Warfare; Weapons
Mining, 21, 22; gold, 87, *map* 90-91; iron, 37; salt, 82, *96-97
Modern art, influence of African art on, *144-145, *164-165, 174
Modigliani, Amedeo, influence of African art on, *144-145
Mogadishu, 88, *map* 91
Mombasa, *map* 9, 88, *map* 91, 180
Monophysite monastery, prayer, *40
Money. *See* Coins; Currencies
Mongol Empire, 84
Monomotapa, Kingdom of, 88, 172
Monsoon, 94
Monteiro, José Maria, 171
Morality, African, 22; sexual, 64, 82; social responsibility basic to, 42; and warfare, 65
Moroccan invasion of Songhai, 81
Morocco, markets in, *98-99
Moslems. *See* Islam; Muslims
Mosques, *24-25, 80; Great Mosque, in Kilwa, *180-181
Mountains, *map* 8-9, *10, 20
Mouse oracle, *124
Mozambique, *map* 91; historical references to region of, 59, 171
Mozambique Channel, *map* 9
Muhammad, Askia. *See* Askia the Great
Murals: in Ethiopian churches, *138-139; Nubian, 39, *41. *See also* Rock paintings
Musawwarat: columns at, *32; elephant frieze at, 37, *38-39
Musa, Mansa, King of Mali, 83-84, *89
Music, 143, 146, 148-149, 174; rhythm, 148, 149-150; Saharan Stone Age peoples, *50, 51
Musical instruments, *50, 107, *112; drums, 146, 148, *149, 150
Muslims: conquest of North Africa, 81; cultural influences of, *24-25, 80, 82, 84, *134-135, 175, *177, *180-181; East African trade, 87, 170; in Egypt, 40, 129; North African trade, *78, 81, *89; North African trade barrier of, 84; religious war in West Africa, 170. *See also* Islam
Mutesa, King of the Ganda, 172
Mutota, King of Monomotapa, 88

N

Naga, 37
Nail fetish, *123
Naletale, stone walls at, *62
Namib Desert, *map* 9, *map* 90
Nana, Chief of Brohimi, 173-174
Napata, *map* 9, *map* 34; Kushite capital, 35, 36, 37
Nastasen, King of Kush, 37
Négritude, 22
Negro ancestry, 20
Nero, Roman Emperor, 38
Netherlands, the. *See* Dutch traders
New Testament, Geez translation of, 42
Ngere mask, *160-161
Nguni peoples, 170
Niani, *map* 90
Niger delta, city-states of, 107, 108; and slave trade, 107
Niger River, *map* 8, *map* 81, *map* 90
Nigeria: Ibo civilization of, 170, 171; Kingdom of Benin, 18, 109 (*see also* Benin); mud hut, *177; Oyo empire, 108, 172; sculpture of, 145, 146, 147-148 (*see also* Benin; Ife; Nok); Yoruba of, 108, 124, 145, 149
Nile River, *map* 9, *map* 34, *map* 81, *map* 91
Nile Valley, settlement of, 33
Noba, nomads, 38, 39, 41, 42
Nobatia, Kingdom of, 39, 40, *41
Nok sculpture, *146, 147
Nomads: infiltration of Kush by, 38, 39; of Libya, 35
North Africa: markets, *98-99; Muslim Arab conquest of, 81; trade, 81-82, 84-85, 86, *map* 90, 91, *92-93
North America, African contributions in: cultural, 168-169; economic, 168
Nuba, 65, *67-77; funeral, *74-77; village, *64-65, *68-69; wrestling, *67, 68, *70-73, 76
Nubia: Christian kingdoms in, 39-40, *41; Egyptian expansion to, 35; Islam in, 40-41
Nubian Desert, *map* 9
Nul, *map* 90
Nyakyusa, 63-64, 66, 172
Nyasa, Lake (Lake Malawi), *map* 9, 66, *map* 91; trading contacts, 88
Nzinga Mbemba, King of Kongo, 101, 105, 107

O

Oases, *map* 90
Oba (King) of Benin, *100, 109, *110-111
Officials: Ashanti, 108; Benin, 109, 111, *116-117; Saharan peoples, *56-57; Songhai, 85
Ohen-Okun, 102
Olduvai Gorge, fossil site, 19
Olodumare, god, 124
Olokun, god, 102
Opobo, kingdom, 108
Oracles, *124
Orange River, *map* 9
Orisha-nla, god, 124
Osei Tutu, Ashanti King, 107, 126
Oyo, kingdom, 108, 172

P

Painting: Ethiopian church murals, *138-139; Ethiopian manuscript, *130-131; Nubian murals, 39, *41; rock, in Sahara, 35, *43-57, 146
Palaces: Ashanti, at Kumasi, 108; of Benin, 18, 104, 109; Husuni Kubwa, Kilwa, 88; Kush, 36; Western Sudanese kingdoms, 24, *26-27, 80
Palm oil industry and trade, Niger delta, 108
Pepper (Malaguetta) Coast, *map* 90, 103
Pepple, King of Bonny, 108
Pereira, Duarte Pacheco, 102

Persia: cultural influence in Ethiopia, 134; Ethiopian trade with, 42
Pharaoh, divinity of, 34
Philip, apostle, 38
Phoenicians, 81
Piaggia, Carlo, 64
Piankhy, King of Kush, 35, 36
Picasso, Pablo, and African art, 144, 165, 174
Plains, fertile, *map* 8-9, *14-15
Political organization, 22, 60, 105, 171. *See also* Law and order; Social order
Polygamy, 64, 85
Porcelain trade, 29, 88, 91
Poro society, 127
Porters, use for transportation of goods, 89, *map* 90-91
Portuguese: in Ethiopia, 42, 129; exploration and trade on African coast, 17, 18, 85, 86, *map* 90-91, 101-102; in Kilwa, *28-29, 88, 180, *182-183; in Monomotapa, 88; relations with Benin, 102, 103; relations with Kongo, 101; slave trade of, 105
Posselt, Willi, 59, 60
Pottery, Kushite, 37
Prester John, 42
Priests and priestesses, 121-122, 125-126
Psammetichus II, King of Egypt, 36
Puberty rites. *See* Initiation ceremonies
Punt, expeditions to, 35
Pygmies, 20, 21, 61-62
Pyramids: of Egypt, 34; of Kush, *14-15, 36
Python, in African religion, 121, *122

Q

Quelimane, *map* 91

R

Racial superiority, European notions of, 60
Rain forests, tropical, *map* 8-9, *10-11; pygmies of, 61-62
Ram, in religion, 34, 37
Ramusio, Giovanni Battista, 86
Rattray, Robert, 125
Records, written, 18, 79-84, *85, 86, 88, 170
Red Noba, 38, 41
Red Sea, *map* 9, 35; Ethiopian influence at southern end of, 41, 42; trade, 37, 87, *map* 91, 94
Religion, African, 121-128; ancestor worship, *122, 126-127, 128, *152; animal worship, 37, 121, *122; of Ashanti, 123-124, 125, 126; basic concepts of, 122-124, 128; of Benin, 112; of Dinka, 123-124; diversity of, 123, 124; fetish worship, 122; High God, 123-124; Kushite, 37; lesser gods, 124, 125-126; Life-Force, concept of, 123, 145, 146, 151; and magic, *table* 125, 127-128; priests and priestesses, 121-122, 125-126; temples and shrines, 124-125. *See also* Christianity; Islam; Sacrifice; Spirit world
Religious art, *120, *142, 143, 145, 147, 148, 150, 151, *152-153, *160-161
Renaissance Europe: and slavery, 106; and witchcraft, 127
Rhodesia: Monomotapa empire, 88, 172; Shona people of, 169; Zimbabwe empire, 59, 62, 88, 178
Rift Valley, *map* 9
Rites of passage, 126. *See also* Initiation ceremonies
Rituals: ancestor worship, 126; and dance, 148, 150, 160; funeral, *74-77; Nuba wrestling, *67, *70-73, 76; Stone Age, in Saharan rock painting, *46-47. *See also* Initiation ceremonies
Roads and Kingdoms, Book of, al-Bakri, 80, 82
Rock paintings, in Sahara, 19, 35, *43-57, 146
Roha, 42

Rome, ancient: contacts with Kush, 37-38; cultural influence in Ethiopia, 134, *135, 137
Rovuma River, *map* 91
Rozwi rulers of Zimbabwe, 88
Rufisque, *map* 90
Ruwenzori Range, *map* 9, *10
Ruyters, Dierick, 104

S

Sabaeans, 41
Sacrifice: of animals, *46-47, 63, *76-77, 122; human, 108, 112, 118
Sahara: desiccation of, 19-20, 36, 43, 46, 55; period of fertility, 19, 34, 43; rock paintings, 19, 35, *43-57, 146; Stone Age peoples of, 33, 34-35, 43, *46-57
Sahara Desert, *map* 8, 9, *10-11, *map* 81; navigation, 93; salt mining in, 82, *96-97; trade across, *78, 81-82, 88, *map* 90-91, *92-93, 105
Sailing routes, *map* 90-91
St. Thomas Aquinas, 105
Saladin, Saracen ruler, 40
Salt mining, 82, *96-97
Salt trade, 81-82, *86, *97
Saracens, in Egypt, 40
Savanna, *map* 8-9, *12-13, 20; period of fertility, 19
Schebesta, Father, 61
Scrub, *map* 8-9, 20
Sculpture, 22, 146-148, *151-165; Ashanti, 22, *106, *152; of Benin, *16, 22, 103, *109-119, 144-145, *147; court, 147 (*see also* Benin; Ife); Dogon, *152, *164-165; Ethiopian, *129; Guro, *151, *156-157; of Ife, 103, 145, *146, 147; impact on Western art, *144-145, *164-165, 174; initial European misjudgment as "primitive," 143-146; Kushite temple frieze, *38-39; Nok, *146, 147; proportions of human figure, 146-147; religious, *120, *142, 143, 145, 147, 148, 150, 151, *152-153, *160-161. *See also* Bronze plaques; Bronze sculpture; Clay sculpture; Masks; Stone sculpture; Wood sculpture
Secrecy imposed on results of early exploration, 21, 85
"Secret societies," 126-127, 160; shrine, *142
Semna, 35
Sena, *map* 91
Senegal, Woloff people of, 101
Senegal River, *map* 8, *map* 90, 102
Senufo people: masks of, 144, 145, 148; shrine, *142
Sex morality, 64, 82
Shabako, King of Kush, 36
Sheba, Queen of, 41, 139, 178
Sheep, domestication of, *46-47
Sherakarer, King of Kush, 39
Shipping, 89; dhows, *28-29, 91, *94-95; Ethiopian, 42; Portuguese, *28, 91; routes, *map* 90-91
Shiva, Hindu god, 37
Shona people, 169
Shrines, communal, 124-125, *142
Shrub, *map* 8-9
Sierra Leone, 102
Sijilmasa, 81, 82, *map* 90, 91
Sixth Dynasty, Egypt, 35
Slave Coast, *map* 90
Slave labor, 105-106; in Americas, 168-169; sacrificial executions, 112
Slave trade, 22; among Africans, 105-106, 107; east coast, 87, 170, 180; effects on African societies, 66, 106-107, 118, 170, 172; Europe and, 105-107; West Africa, 85, 102, 103, 104, 105-107, 118, 172
Sleeping sickness, 20, 21
Snake, in African religion, 121, *122
Social order and organization, 21, 22, 60-66, 169, 174; age patterns, 63-64; captive labor and slavery, 105-106; of Dinka, 62-63, 169, 172; Ethiopian feudalism, 42; kinship patterns, 60, 63, 65, 66, 106; of Nyakyusa, 63-64, 172; morality determined by adherence to,

42; role of ancestor cults in, 126, 128; role of "secret societies," 126-127; of Saharan Stone Age peoples, *56-57; of Tallensi, 65-66, 172; of Tonga, 66, 172; trading kingdoms and cities, 22, 79-84, 88, 103, 104, 105, 108, 109, 171-172; village societies, 22, *56-57, 60-66, 172, 175. See also Law and order
Social welfare, 21
Sofala, map 9, 88, map 91, 180
Solomon, King, 41, 139, 178
Solomonid dynasty in Ethiopia, 41, 131, 139
Somali Peninsula, map 9
Somalia, historical reference to region of, 87
Songhai, Kingdom of, 22, 79-80, map 81, 84; dates of existence of, 81; description by Leo Africanus, 79, 85; trade, 81, 86
Songs, 146, 150
Sorcery, 127-128
Spain, legalization of slave trade by, 106
Spice trade, 91, 102, 103, 104
Spirit world, 123, 160; ancestors, 60, 123, 126-127, 153; communication with, *74, 125; deities, 125-126; sculptured "spirit homes," *152-153; unborn generations, 60, 123, 153
Stanley, Henry Morton, 172
Steppe, semiarid, map 8-9
Stone Age, 21, 146; peoples remaining on level of, 61-62; Saharan peoples, 33, 34-35, 43, *46-57; Saharan rock paintings, 35, *43-57, 146
Stone sculpture, 147-148
Storytelling, art of, 143, 150
Sudan: Dinka of, 62-63, 123-124, 169, 172; Egyptian expansion to, 35; Kushite civilization in, 35-38; Kushite pyramids in, *14-15; Nuba of, *64-65, *67-77; Zande of, 64-65, 127-128. See also Central Sudan; Western Sudan
Sudan, Republic of the, 67
Sudd, map 9
Surrealism, 165
Swahili, language, 29
Swastikas, as ornamentation of Ethiopian churches, *134-135

T

Taghaza, 82, map 90, 97
Taharqa, King of Kush, 36
Takedda, map 90, 91
Talismans, 125
Talking drum, *149
Tallensi, 65-66, 172; religion of, 127
Tanganyika. See Tanzania
Tanganyika, Lake, map 9, map 91
Tangier, map 90
Tanuatanum, King of Kush, 36
Tanzania: anthropological fossil finds in,

19; historical references to region of, 87, 94; Nyakyusa of, 63-64. See also Zanzibar
Tarikh al-Fettash, al-Kati, 79
Tassili n'Ajjer plateau, map 8, 43, 45; Stone Age rock paintings, *44-57
Tattooing, 154
Technological simplicity, 22, 108, 169
Tegguida N'Tisemt, salt mining, *96
Temples: communal, 124-125, *142; Great, at Zimbabwe, 59, *61, *62, 88, *178-179; Kushite, 37, *38-39
Terra-cotta sculpture, 145, *146, 147, 148
Tete, map 91
Textiles industry, Kano, 172-173
Textiles trade, 29, 86, 88, 91, 103, 104-105, 172
Thebes, map 34; Kushite seizure of, 35
Thomassey, Paul, 80
Thutmose I, King of Egypt, 35
Tibesti Massif, map 8
Timbuktu, map 8, *24-25, 26, 79, 84, 85, 86, map 90, 91; book trade, 17-18, 84
Tlemcen, map 90
Togo, historical reference to region of, 107
Tonga, 66, 172
Tools and utensils: artistry in, *106, *154-157, *162-163; bronze and copper, vs. iron, 36; counterweight, *106; household, *162-163; iron, 21, 36, *58; sense of form and function, 162; Stone Age, Hunter period, 46
Tortoise-shell trade, 87
Touré, Samori ibn Lafiya, 79
Touré, Sékou, 79
Towerson, Captain, 102
Towns. See Cities and towns
Trade, 21, 89, 173; book, Timbuktu, 17-18, 84; copper, 88; East African coastal cities, *28-29, 37, 41, 86, 87-88, map 91, *94-95, 105, 180; Egyptian, 35; Ethiopian, 41, 42, 134; European, with North and West Africa, *23, 84-86, map 90, 91, 101, 102-103, 104-107; gems, 29, 88, 91; gold, 29, 81-82, 85, 86-87, 88, 91, 94, 107; inland, central Africa, 18, 88, 89, map 90-91; iron, 29, 87, 88; ivory, 29, 42, *86, 87, 88, 91, 94, 102; kingdoms of West African coastal and forest regions, map 90, 91, 101, 102-103, 104-107, 108, *116-117; kingdoms of Western Sudan, *78, 81-82, 84-87, *89, map 90, 91, 105, 107; Kushite (Meroitic), 37, 38; marketplaces, *98-99; palm oil, 108; porcelain, 29, 88, 91; role of "secret societies" in, 127; salt, 81-82, *86, *97; slave, 22, 85, 87, 102, 103, 104, 105-107, 118, 170, 172, 180; spices, 91, 102, 103, 104; textiles, 29, 86, 88, 91, 102, 104-105, 172; tortoise shell, 87; trans-Saharan, *78, 81-82, 88, map 90-91, *92-93, 105; various products, 29, 88, 89, 91, 94, 104-105, 116
Trade routes, map 90-91, 92
Traditionalism, African, 169-170, 172-

174; in art, 143, 145, 148, *156-157
Transportation of goods, means of, 89, map 90-91. See also Camel; Shipping
Tripoli, map 8, map 90
Tropical rain forests. See Rain forests
Tsetse fly, *20
Tuaregs, in camel caravan, *92-93
Tuat, 85, map 90
Tunis, map 90
Turnbull, Colin, 62

U

Uganda, historical references to region of, 37, 172
Ukwangala, fireside fellowship, 63

V

Vaal River, map 9
Van Velsen, Jaap, 66
Venice, and African trade, 84
Victoria, Lake, map 9, map 91
Victoria Falls, map 9, map 90
Village societies, 22, 60-66, 175; Dinka, 62-63, 169, 172; Nuba, *67-77; Nyakyusa, 63-64, 172; Saharan Stone Age, 43, *46-57; Tallensi, 65-66, 172; Tonga, 66, 172
Villages, 177; Chad, *176-177; Nuba, *64-65, *68-69; Saharan Stone Age peoples, *48-49

W

Walata, map 8, 82, map 90, 91
Warfare: Benin, *118-119; Bornu, *30-31; European misconceptions about prevalence of, among African tribes, 64-65; Saharan peoples, *54-55; slave raids, 107, 172; use of elephants, 37; Zande, 64-65. See also Military power; Weapons
Wargla, map 90
Water-raising device, Sahara, Stone Age, *49
Wawat, under Egyptian control, 35
Weapons, 21; Benin, *110, *116-117; Bornu, *30-31; bronze vs. iron, 36; hunting, *114-115; of Saharan Stone Age herdsmen, *54-55
Welfare, social, 21
West Africa: cities of coastal and forest regions, 18, 101-102, 103-104, 107-108, 109, 118; cultural similarities with Egypt, 34; European colonialism in, 108, 167-168; kingdoms of coastal and forest regions, 101-102, 103-105, 107-108, *109-119, 172; Muslim religious

war in, 170; Portuguese exploration of coast of, 85, 101, 102; sculpture of, *16, 22, 103, *106, *109-119, *142, 144, *145-147, 148, *151-165; slave trade, 85, 102, 103, 104, 105-107; trade, *78, 81-82, 84-87, *89, map 90, 91, *92-93, 101, 102-103, 104-107, 108, *116-117. See also Western Sudan
West Indies slave trade, 103
Western Sudan: cities of, 17-18, *24-27, 79, 80, 81, 82, 84, 85, 86; Islam in, 27, 80, 82, 84, 103; kingdoms of, 79-80, map 81, 82-84, 101, 103, 105, 172; trade, *78, 81-82, 84-87, *89, map 90, 91, 105, 107
Wilson, Monica, 63, 64
Witch doctors, 127-128
Witchcraft, 127-128; comparisons with Europe, 105, 127, 128
Woloff people, military power of, 101
Women, *16, 27, *74, 82, *111; priestesses, 121-122, 125; Saharan Stone Age peoples, *48-53
Wood sculpture, *142, 143-144, 148, *151-165
Wrestling, among Nuba, *67, 68, *70-73, 76
Writing: Kushite (Meroitic), 36, 37; Sabaean, 41
Wut, Dinka cattle camp, 63

X

X-Group culture, 39

Y

Yamvo, Mwata, 171
Yellow fever, 20
Yoruba people, 146; kingdom of (Oyo), 108, 172; religion of, 124; sculpture of (Ife), 103, 145, *146, 147; talking drum of, *149

Z

Zagwe dynasty, Ethiopia, 131, 139
Zambezi River, map 9, map 90-91
Zambia, historical reference to region of, 88
Zande, 64-65; religion of, 127-128
Zanzibar, map 9, map 91, 180; slave trade, 170
Zeila, map 91
Zimbabwe, map 9, 22, 59-60, 66, 88, 178; Great Temple, 59, *61, *62, 88, *178-179; Monomotapa dynasty, 88, 172; Rozwi dynasty, 88; trade center, 88, map 91, 180
Zuila, map 90

Printed in U.S.A.